→» 52 «←
DATES
FOR YOU
AND YOUR
MATE

Dave and Claudia Arp

THOMAS NELSON PUBLISHERS
Nashville

Other Books by the Authors

THE MARRIAGE TRACK
BEATING THE WINTER BLUES
SANITY IN THE SUMMERTIME
60 ONE-MINUTE MARRIAGE BUILDERS
60 ONE-MINUTE FAMILY BUILDERS
60 ONE-MINUTE MEMORY MAKERS

Copyright © 1993 by Dave and Claudia Arp

Published in Nashville, Tennessee, by Thomas Nelson, Inc.,
Publishers, and distributed in Canada by Word
Communications, Ltd., Richmond, British Columbia, and in the
United Kingdom by Word (UK), Ltd., Milton Keynes, England.

Library of Congress Cataloging-in-Publication Data

Arp, Dave.
      52 dates for you and your mate / Dave and Claudia Arp.
          p.   cm.
      ISBN 0-8407-3435-2
      1. Marriage—United States.   2. Dating (Social customs)
3.   Man-woman relationships—United States. I. Arp,
Claudia.   II. Title.   III. Title: Fifty two dates for you and
your mate.
HQ734.A686 1993
306.872—dc20   92-20484
                                                              CIP

Printed in the United States of America

      5   6 - 97   96   95

Contents

DO IT TOGETHER DATES

CHEAP AND EASY DATES

"WE'RE JUST TOO TIRED" DATES

THE BEST DATES FROM MARRIAGE ALIVE ALUMNI

To couples everywhere who want to add fun to their marriage through dating.

W e are grateful to our friends, family members, and participants in our Marriage Alive Workshops who shared their creative dates with us so we could pass them on to you.

Special thanks to Janie Johnson for her help; to our two favorite editors, Janet Thoma and Susan Salmon; and to the in-house staff of Thomas Nelson who make writing fun for us.

Foreword

"**M**any view marriage as death, boredom, or the end of the line," a marriage specialist said on a recent television talk show. It made us stop and question, "Why are people frightened of marriage? Why do some view it as the 'end of the line?' "

Having worked with married couples for many years, we have our own opinion. We believe life goes out of a marriage when the couple stops working on it. To take it a step further, we have observed that when a couple stops working on their marriage, they stop having fun together. Show us a marriage that is faltering, and we'll show you a marriage where the fun is gone.

And where the fun is gone, there is a mighty good chance they don't date their mate! Dating is something they did before they got married. It is not in their marriage vocabulary today.

In the following pages, we want to do something about that. We offer you 52 Dates for You and Your Mate. Unlike books you read from cover to cover, you can read this book spontaneously. Simply read the section that suits your present mood; then choose a date from that section. Remember this is a resource to enrich your relationship with each other.

This book is divided into seven parts, each offering a

different category of dates. You'll find everything from Romantic Dates to Getting in Shape Dates to Cheap and Easy Dates. We especially recommend the "We're Just Too Tired" Dates for those times you think you're just too exhausted to date your mate.

We want to emphasize that all the dates in this book have been done by someone, somewhere! A big thank you to all those who shared their creative dates with us. Many are alumni from our Marriage Alive Workshops all around the country. From Washington State to Florida, they happily pass their fun times on to you.

Will dating make a difference in your marriage? Our answer is an emphatic "Yes!" If you don't believe us, ask Fred and Nancy. Here's what they wrote us:

"Thank you for sharing your dating ideas. My husband and I have a lot of fun in our marriage and it is legal, moral, and inexpensive. We know we can't take our marriage for granted, so we continue to search for reinforcements such as your books."

Fred and Nancy, here is the next installment! This book is for you and for all who want to make their marriages come alive with fun, laughter, and good times together. The ball is in your court. Go on and have a great time dating your mate!

Just for Fun Dates

1 ♥ Formal Dinner in the Park Date

The Idea: Formal dinners don't have to be stuffy and don't have to be crowded affairs. Actually, the guest list can include only two—you and your mate. There is no real protocol for this date. It's completely open-ended but our friends, Larry and Lois, tell us it's a ball.

Make Your Mate Feel Like a Star: Most everyone has been to a picnic in a park—complete with paper plates, cold fried chicken, plenty of people, and ants and other bugs. But very few have attended a private black-tie affair out under the stars. This is one date, if you pull it off, that will make your mate feel like a star celebrity.

Choose the Right Setting: Choose a park that lends itself to the romantic like one with a waterfall, statues, or maybe a lake. It's easy to convert a picnic table into a formal dining room, or you can bring your own folding table and chairs. You'll also need to bring your favorite tablecloth, linen napkins, china, and silverware. A vase of fresh flowers (wildflowers are ideal) and a candelabra will add to the formal atmosphere.

If you are industrious, you can prepare food beforehand and grill in the park (if allowed). Or if you want to simplify, call your favorite restaurant and order take-out dinners. Another option is to pick up dinner from the deli at your favorite gourmet grocery store.

Dress for the Occasion: You will want to dress appropriately. Put on your tux or formal gown if you already own one, but prepare yourself for a few stares. If you don't want to go that formal, a coat and tie or dress is fine and will still add to the formality of the evening.

Take along a boom box with your favorite music tapes or CDs to add to the atmosphere. If you feel nostalgic, we suggest oldies music from your pre-marriage dates. If you're looking for something fresh and romantic in an outdoorsy way, we recommend:

- A favorite classical recording.
- George Winston (piano and instrumental from Windom Hill).
- Michael Hedges (wonderful acoustical guitar).

This might be just the opportunity to surprise your date with a new CD or tape—one that will remind you of your Formal Dinner in the Park Date.

Consider Alternatives: An option for those who do not live near a park: Our son and daughter-in-law, Joel and Jeanne, set up a table, complete with tablecloth and candles on their front walk. Not only did they experience a unique and fun dinner—they also provided their neighbors with a new topic of conversation and laughter.

2 ♥ Photo Date

The Idea: We love pictures! In fact we spent the first year of our empty nest going through all our pictures, framing and hanging the special ones.

Perhaps you've heard of a "Wailing Wall." Well we have a "Wedding Wall," with pictures dating back to our parents as well as pictures from our two married children. Actually it was our last family wedding that instigated our Photo Dates. Looking at Jeanne and Joel's pictures of their honeymoon, we were amazed at how many pictures they had of just the two of them. When we asked who took the pictures, we discovered they were the photographers. They simply set the timer on their camera and ran and posed for their self-portraits.

Learn to Do It Right: At the next opportunity, we had our own Photo Date. We didn't have immediate success. We didn't even know how to set the timer on our camera! When we finally figured it out, we didn't always focus it right. Only the two of us know who the black shadows are in some of the pictures. But we did have fun in the process and are continuing to fine-tune our Photo Dates. Now with our empty-nest pictures, we have some of the two of us that hold happy memories. So happy, that we suggest you have your own Photo Date.

Adapt the Date for You: You will need to adapt this date to your own situation. If you have a camera with a timer, all the better. If not, you can buy inexpensive extension cables to trigger the camera for couple self-portraits. Just remember, for every great shot you take, you'll shoot four or five others.

Keep Your Costs Down: The cost of developing film has come down in recent years. Research your own area and find the cheapies. Look for discount coupons in your local newspaper or special deals at your grocery store. Our favorite and cheapest place also offers one-hour service which is great for those of us who like immediate gratification!

If you don't have a camera with a timer, or don't even have a camera, you can pick up an inexpensive disposable camera (which includes film) for about six dollars. Even adding the cost of developing, your date should not cost over ten dollars, which makes this date a Cheap and Easy Date too.

Go to your favorite haunts and snap away. You may even be able to recruit an unsuspecting person to snap a picture of the two of you together.

You can extend the fun of this date by making your own memory scrapbook. You'll be cataloging memories together. Picture that!

3 ♥ Owl-Watching Date

The Idea: The Owl-Watching Date may be the most unique date we've heard.

While participating in a Book Fest, we picked up this creative date from a fellow author, Fred Alsop. Sitting with other authors in the "signing well" and waiting for the autograph seekers to arrive gave us the opportunity to visit with Fred. Our standard question, "What is your favorite date?" received anything but a standard answer. Fred's suggestion? Have an Owl-Watching Date! Looking for owls on a moonlit night, he tried to convince us, can be romantic as well as fun.

Prepare for the Night: Now we promised you that someone has actually done each of our fifty-two dates, and Fred swore he had done the Owl-Watching Date many, many times. His suggestions included the following:

1. Choose a moonlit, warm night with no time limitations.

2. Find a quiet place. The more secluded the location the better, but Fred told us if you are a city slicker, you can do this date in your own backyard or local park.

3. Be patient. Sometimes owls will appear in as little as twenty minutes. Sometimes you may need to wait several hours. But it's amazing, he told us, how being alone to-

gether in the dark, out in nature, causes wonderful con-
versations to happen. Subjects you haven't talked about
for years may surface. Simple things remembered are
likely to bring a closeness that just doesn't happen in the
hustle and bustle of the day.

4. To increase your chance of seeing owls, try imitating
them. To illustrate, Fred gave us a piercing Screech Owl
call. (We'll have to practice that one.)

5. To learn more about owls, or other birds as well,
pick up and study a book on birds. If you live in the
southeastern part of the USA, we recommend Fred's
book, *Birds of the Smokies* (Great Smoky Mountain Natural History Association: Gatlinburg, TN, 1991).

6. To top off your Owl-Watching Date, here's one last
suggestion from Fred: As the sun comes up, cook breakfast together.

We're not real outdoorsy people, but this is one date we
just may try. Since Dave's a "night owl" and Claudia's a
"day lark," we at least would see a couple of "birds." Who
knows what other fun things we might find to do!

4 ♥ Gourmet Cooking Date

The Idea: Some dates you have before you get married seem to be natural dates after you get married too. Our own married kids have proven this in our family. We've even been the recipients of their Gourmet Cooking Dates. This Arp date has a history.

When our kids were in college, their funds for gourmet restaurants were limited but their taste for fine cuisine was not! So they began to cook their own gourmet dinners. A fun Arp tradition evolved. Whenever our sons had college friends to visit in our home, they sequestered their unsuspecting guests into culinary duty. Whoever was visiting (male or female), joined forces with our kids and cooked a special dinner. One of their friends, Chris, turned out to be a first-class French chef.

Choose a Theme: Sometimes these dinners had themes. We never knew quite what to expect—like the time Jarrett and Laurie did an Oriental dinner. They served us on the screened porch on a quilt surrounded by plants. We felt we were in an Oriental garden.

Have Fun Breaking Tradition: The most memorable gourmet meal from Jeanne and Joel was the Christmas before they were married. Their Christmas gift to our family was to prepare the entire Christmas dinner.

That year tradition was out and gourmet was in. It was an experience we won't soon forget. They cooked straight through the night on Christmas Eve. Have you ever tried to sleep to the smells and sounds of making homemade manicotti?

You Can Plan Your Dinner: If you have never

had a Gourmet Cooking Date and are interested in trying one, here are a few pointers:

1. Choose recipes you've never cooked before. A good source of recipes is *Gourmet—The Magazine of Good Living* or *Bon Appetit.* You can have a fun preliminary date reading all those cookbooks you got as wedding presents or purchased through fund raisers.

2. Together make out your grocery list. You may want to set a budget for your meal, but go on and be a little extravagant. It definitely will be a cheaper date than going to an exclusive gourmet restaurant.

3. Grocery shop together. This can be another fun preliminary date.

While this is a fun Just-for-Two Date, you may want to turn it into an even more productive date by pulling off the Dinner Party Date (see page 73).

Choose from Our Family Favorites: Here

are some of our family's favorite sources of recipes.

From Joel & Jeanne who love to cook Italian:
> *Pasta Fresca* (New York: William Morrow, 1988).
> *Cucina Rustica* (New York: William Morrow, 1990).

From Jarrett and Laurie whose specialty is vegetarian:
> *Sundays at Moosewood Restaurant* (New York: Simon
> & Schuster, 1990).

The Vegetarian Epicure Book II, Anna Thomas (New York: Alfred A. Knopf, 1972).

From Dave and Claudia who like to cook "easy":

Cuisine Rapide, Pierre Franey & Bryan Miller (New York: Random House, 1989).

Cookbooks by Pierre Franey including: *60 Minute Gourmet* (New York: Fawcett Columbine, 1979) and *More 60 Minute Gourmet* (New York: Times Books, 1981).

The Mom's Support Group Cookbook (100 Easy and Fun Recipes from Busy Moms), Marriage Alive International, 1992. May be ordered from Marriage Alive, P.O. Box 90303, Knoxville, TN 37990. (Send $9.95 which includes shipping and handling.)

From our son Jonathan, the college student who likes to eat, and is beginning to like to cook, here is his favorite recipe that he found on the package of egg spaghetti. With his unique modifications (he used two whole heads of garlic for two cloves of garlic) we had a most interesting and very tasty dish. It's become one of our family's favorites. Here is the recipe:

Italiano Marinara

2 tablespoons olive oil
1 medium onion, chopped
2 cloves garlic, minced (More garlic actually added zest!)
3 1/2 cups (28 oz. can) tomatoes, undrained
2 tablespoons chopped fresh parsley (Jonathan used dried parsley and added more.)
2 teaspoons basil

1 teaspoon sugar
1/2 teaspoon oregano
1/2 teaspoon salt
1/4 teaspoon pepper (He suggests fresh ground
    pepper.)
1 package (8 oz.) Pastamania® Pesto Spaghetti,
    uncooked
1 cup (4 oz) shredded mozzarella cheese. (Jonathan
    added more cheese as well.)

In a 2-quart saucepan heat oil and cook onion and garlic until tender but not brown. Stir in tomatoes with liquid, parsley, sugar, basil, oregano, salt and pepper; bring to a boil then reduce heat and simmer, stirring occasionally to break up tomatoes, 15 - 20 minutes. Meanwhile, cook spaghetti according to package directions, drain. Toss spaghetti with sauce and place in 1-quart casserole. Top with mozzarella cheese and broil 3 minutes or until cheese is melted.

Makes 4 servings.

5 ♥ Bubble Date

The Idea: Sometimes our neighbors worry about us! On this day they were really concerned. "What are the Arps up to now?" they asked, as they watched humongous bubbles floating over the roof of our house.

"Not to worry," we could have told them. We were simply having a Bubble Date!

One perk (or liability) of our work in marriage and family enrichment is we get to try out ideas before passing them on to others. That's how we came to have a Bubble Date. But it was so much fun, we have repeated it several times.

A friend put a bug in our ears that blowing bubbles—big bubbles—was lots of fun. We did have positive childhood memories of little plastic containers of liquid and the fun of making bubbles, so we decided to give the big bubbles a try. You can too!

Get What You Need: The equipment is simple. You can pick up large commercial bubble wands in toy stores. They come in an assortment of astro-bright colors and sizes. Or you can make your own wands out of coat hangers.

Follow the Recipe: Make your own bubble mixture with this simple recipe:

Bubble Fun

Combine:
  2 cups liquid detergent
  3/4 cup corn syrup
  6 cups water

Put bubble mixture in a large shallow pan—like a roasting pan. Dip the bubble wand and wave through the air. You'll have wonderful large bubbles everywhere. You also can use a kitchen funnel. Dip the large end of the funnel into the bubble mixture and blow through the small end.

Take the Idea Everywhere: By the way, this is definitely an out-of-doors date and one you'll find yourself wanting to repeat. It's especially fun at the beach. You can watch as the beach winds take your bubbles to parts unknown.

For other fun, uninhibited date activities, look in books of activities for children like *Sanity in the Summertime* by Linda Dillow and Claudia Arp (Thomas Nelson, Revised 1991) and *Beating the Winter Blues* by Claudia Arp (Thomas Nelson, 1991).

There's a child in each of us. Be willing to let your child out from time to time. It will add laughter and fun to your marriage team.

6 ♥ Coupon Date

Dr. Scott Peck, in his bestseller book, *The Road Less Traveled* (New York: Simon & Schuster, 1978), says a sign of maturity is to be able to delay gratification. The Coupon Date lets you do just that—but you get to have fun in the process.

Remember all those fun things you occasionally talk about but never get around to doing? Now is an opportunity to put some feet on those good ideas. Or perhaps you want to do something fun together but have difficulty coming up with anything to do. If this fits you, we just may have the solution to your dilemma. Have a Coupon Date!

The Idea: Coupon Dates began to appear at the Arps' when our children were young. We were so busy with family, careers, and other activities that our date times together were practically nonexistent. We decided to do something about it by having a Coupon Date.

Just what is a Coupon Date? It's a date to come up with future dates—thus Dr. Peck's "delayed gratification." But it is also fun.

Brainstorm Date Ideas: Part of the fun of dating your mate is the anticipation factor—looking forward to the things you are going to do together. Here's how to begin.

1. Choose a time when you won't be interrupted for a couple of hours. You may want to go out for breakfast or coffee and dessert. Take along pen and paper and your imagination.

2. You can draw from our fifty-two date suggestions or come up with others like:

- Go roller skating.
- Fly kites together.
- Catch your favorite movie.
- Watch the sunset, sunrise, etc.
- Fill in with your own idea: _____.

3. Now make the date coupons. Here's what you need:

- Index cards
- Hole puncher
- Colored markers
- Yarn

Punch a hole in each card. (If you are artsy, you can decorate each card.) Write out one date idea for each coupon. Tie coupons together with yarn and presto, you have a coupon book for future dates.

One final suggestion: Hang your coupon book in a conspicuous place, perhaps in the kitchen so you will see it often. It will be a reminder of fun times ahead. Who says delayed gratification isn't fun? Not us, but this is one date you won't want to delay.

7 ♥ Book Date

The Idea: Two of our favorite activities are eating and reading, so when we discovered a bookstore that served food, we knew we had hit the jackpot. More and more bookstores are becoming innovative in what they offer, so check out the bookstores in your local area.

One friend from Nashville, Tennessee, told us about a bookstore where you can go and listen to poetry readings. One of our favorite bookstores offers unique opportunities like mini-workshops on travel to autograph sessions with authors. They also offer Story Time for children. We know couples who take their young children to Story Time and then have fun browsing through books while their little ones are happily entertained.

Reading You Can Do Together: Another couple, Nan and Randy, enjoy reading the same book or chapter and then discussing it when they go out for breakfast or dinner. If you are looking for books to read together which will enrich your life and marriage, consider the following:

- *How to Have a Happy Marriage* by David and Vera Mace (Nashville: Abingdon, 1977).
- *The Road Less Traveled* by M. Scott Peck (New York: Simon & Schuster, 1978).

- *The Marriage Track* by Dave and Claudia Arp (Nashville: Thomas Nelson, 1992).
- *60 One-Minute Marriage Builders* by Dave and Claudia Arp (Nashville: Wolgemuth & Hyatt, 1989).
- *Passages of Marriage* by Dr. Frank and Mary Alice Minirth, Dr. Brian and Dr. Debborah Newman, and Dr. Robert and Susan Hemfelt (Nashville: Thomas Nelson, 1991).
- *7 Habits of Highly Effective People* by Stephen R. Covey (New York: A Fireside Book, Simon & Schuster, 1989).

This is one date that not only is fun, but can pump some fresh air into your marital tires. It's your turn to prove that we are right. Go on and book your Book Date. Trust us. You won't be disappointed.

8 ♥ Yellow Road, Blue Highways Date

Dave's travel motto is, "Why travel on the interstate if there is a cute yellow road you can take?" Claudia's travel motto is, "How quickly can we get there, and which is the most direct route?" Obviously, we have very different travel perspectives, but there is one time we do agree. It's when we have a Yellow Road Date!

The Idea: What's a yellow road? Dave's little yellow roads became famous when we were living in Austria. Whenever we traveled, he always wanted to take the scenic route. We soon learned that on the Austrian maps, yellow roads meant scenery—gorgeous scenery! We also learned that yellow roads could mean narrow roads (as in room for one car on a mountain ledge) or gravel roads. On one unforgettable occasion, it meant a cow path. Traveling Austria's yellow roads in our American station wagon was very interesting. We still wonder how we were able to navigate some of them.

Over the years of traveling yellow roads we have seen a lot of beautiful country, so we confidently recommend this date to you, especially since another couple, Brenda and Mike, made the same dating suggestion. They actually called their date a Blue Highways Date, which they named for the book by William Least Heat-Moon, *Blue*

Highways. Here are their tips on how to have a Blue Highways Date.

Plan to Travel the Backroads:

1. Consider how much time you have for your Blue Highways Date. Brenda and Mike suggest a minimum of one day. If you can make it an overnight or weekend, all the better.

2. Choose the area you'd like to explore. For instance, in California, it might be the San Bernardino Mountains or Redwood Forest; in New York, the Catskills, or in Colorado, the Rockies. It could even be a forty mile radius around your own home town.

3. Go to an unfamiliar area and take the little blue roads. No interstate travel or four lane roads are allowed.

4. Resist the urge to stop at fast food or chain restaurants. See what you can discover. Stop at any interesting place you find. Once on an Arp Yellow Road Date we stopped in the backroads of the backroads to get gas. The lady at the checkout counter had already mellowed out with a big wad of chewing tobacco in one side of her mouth.

Discover New Territories: You never know what you may find. Brenda and Mike said they've discovered everything from pig races to barbecues. Once, they even stopped for a square dance.

We've stumbled onto wonderful museums, parks, nature trails, antique shops, and junk stores. Did you know that in the mountains of North Carolina, they even have "wooly worm races"? It's an annual event and people come from all over. We've also found quaint little Bed and

Breakfasts and property where we would love to build a mountain cabin. (That's for our fantasy date!)

Perhaps most enjoyable is the beautiful scenery we've discovered. Sometimes we like just to get out of the car, sit on a rock or log, and realize how thankful we are for this unique, beautiful world and for giving us each other. Maybe we should retitle the date, The Grateful Date. Try it and see if you agree!

Getting in Shape
Dates

9 ♥ Walk and Talk Date

This may well be Claudia's all-time favorite Getting in Shape Date as she likes to both walk and talk! Dave is a good listener and needs the exercise too, so several times each week you will find us walking and talking.

The Idea: Over the years we've discovered that our Walk and Talk Dates are quite productive. Many times when we are in the middle of writing a chapter or article and we're fresh out of creativity, we are able to get back on track if we walk and talk about it. If walking causes your creative juices to flow, take a tip from us and bring along an index card and pencil. We find if we don't write down our ideas, we've forgotten them by the time we get home.

Learn the Benefits: To be honest, we can't think of any other kind of date that is as good for our health and our communication as our Walk and Talk Dates. They're cheap and easy. And they're simple. If you are the spontaneous type, this may just be the date for you. It requires no planning, unless you have small children and have to arrange for a baby-sitter. And because you can walk just about anywhere, you can have these dates anytime.

Choose Your Favorite Stomping Grounds:

It's also a flexible date. You can walk just about anywhere. Some of our favorite walking places are:

- Would you believe, around our block? It's approximately 1/2 mile so if we walk around the block four times, we will have walked approximately two miles. It's also easy. We don't have to get in the car and drive anywhere.
- Nature trails and mountain paths. More planning and time are needed but it's worth it.
- Shopping malls. Many open early to accommodate local walkers. Claudia enjoys walking in malls more than Dave. He doesn't complain as long as the stores are closed since shopping together reminds him of the Cherokee's Trail of Tears!
- Historic areas. Many cities and towns have a historic section. Sometimes you can even find a guidebook. This is a great date for history buffs.
- Outdoor tracks. We like to walk on a track around a couple of soccer fields. It reminds us of one advantage of the empty nest—no soccer practices! With three sons, we lived through thirteen years of soccer games and practices. It's not that we didn't enjoy those years, but we did pay our dues.
- Walking and biking paths. You don't have to watch out for cars—just bikes!
- The beach. This is our all-time favorite place to walk.

Add your favorite walking places to our list and get ready for a fun way to stay in shape. This date, while great for your health, will help keep your marriage fit too!

10 ♥ Bike Date

Since we wrote about our Biking Dates in *The Marriage Track,* we have heard from several readers about their Getting in Shape Bike Dates. One couple told us about a cross-country foliage biking tour in the hills of Vermont. Here's what Dan and Leah said.

The Idea: "For our tenth anniversary we decided to take an October bike tour of Vermont. The leaves were incredible. It's amazing how much more dramatic they are when you are out in the open air seeing them than when you see them from inside your car. Our first experience was so exhilarating that we repeated it for our eleventh anniversary."

They skipped last year but tell us they are headed back to Vermont this fall for their third bike tour. That is quite an endorsement, so we asked more questions.

Plan for the Essentials: "Where do you stay at night?" we asked. This was a key question for us as we used all our camping out energy when our three sons were growing up.

"Oh," Leah answered, "we stay at quaint little country inns." She immediately had our attention.

"But what about your clothes and baggage?" Claudia asked, being the practical one. We then discovered the tour provides a van to take your luggage from one inn to the next.

"Biking makes me awfully hungry. Where do you eat lunch?" Dave inquired.

Dan cleared that one up. "We receive instructions each morning. They tell us what route to take and where to stop for lunch. It's usually at a little gourmet inn or teahouse. The food is wonderful, and the morning of biking gives you the appetite to appreciate it. Because you're burning so many calories, you don't have to watch what you eat. The tour also tells us what to look for as well as where we will be staying that evening. Everything is taken care of. They provide bikes, helmets, and drinking water. They are even prepared to fix flat tires.

"We have two guides and a support van close by. It is a group tour, but the group is small and it's fun to meet other couples from around the country. The group is so diverse that we don't spend a lot of time talking about children and, in a way, that's nice."

Leah added that the best part for her was being alone with Dan without their children and not having to worry about preparing meals. She loved being able to talk without interruptions or simply to be quiet.

Write for More Information: By this time they really had our interest. We learned there are week-long tours as well as weekend tours. We also filed away the name of their tour group and will include it for your information:

VCC Four Seasons Cycling
P.O. Box 145

Waterbury Center, VT 05677-0145
Telephone: 802-244-5135

For more information you could write or call:

Vermont Chamber of Commerce
Department of Travel and Tourism
P.O. Box 37
Montpelier, VT 05601
Telephone: 802-223-3443

Consider Alternatives: We realize this date is
one of the super splurge suggestions. If these trips don't
fit your budget or your schedule but you want to bike
together, you can plan your own trip, even for a day near
your home. You can pack a lunch and rent two bikes and
ride through your local park. It isn't exactly the same as a
week of biking in Vermont, but take it from us, it's fun! We
know because we've done it. Maybe next year we can try
Vermont!

11 ♥ New Sport Date

We'll never forget our most traumatic sports date—our first adventure on snow skis. Recently, we read that the beginning skier needs "adventure in the soul, bravery in the heart, strength in the body—and brakes." When we had our first New Sport Date, learning to ski, twenty years ago, we qualified for adventure, bravery, and strength—but the "brakes" part was missing!

The Idea: We were living in southern Germany and most everybody skied—or so our friends told us—as they presented us with their old, used skis. Knowing nothing about skiing, we didn't know our gift skis were so ancient that they should have been in a ski museum—not on our feet. Dave was the first to discover they had no brakes as he not so gracefully fell between two sign posts and slid under the sign. We quickly learned that the only way to stop is to fall, sit down, or hit something—or someone.

Our first New Sport Date obviously was not that successful. But we are adventurous at heart and we did live right in the middle of Ski Country, so our tenacity won out. After a few lessons and lots of practice, we found we were enjoying skiing more and falling less. We even learned how to "snowplow" and come to a complete stop without hitting another skier.

One thing that motivated us to stick with it was the

number of senior citizens we saw on the ski slopes. We felt certain that if they could ski, we should be able to ski. (They also got discounted tickets—something for us to look forward to someday.) Skiing was also a hit with our three sons, who at one time or another all raced competitively.

Save Yourself Some Pain: If you are even thinking about a ski date as your New Sport Date, let us save you the pain and suffering we've experienced with the following suggestions.

1. Ski equipment is more important than ski clothes. Start with short skis. Our first skis towered way above our heads and looked more like skis for ski jumping. Claudia wore bright orange, so if she fell or wandered off the beaten path, she could be found. She didn't think about how conspicuous she would look or how self-conscious she would feel on the slopes in her bright orange.

2. Take lessons! Unless you are a kid or are extremely athletic, it will not come naturally. A good ski instructor can help you enjoy this date faster, better, and safer.

3. Don't overdress. We can remember feeling like mummies with all our extra socks, underwear, turtle necks, sweaters, jackets, hats, ear muffs, and gloves. No wonder we couldn't get up when we fell. We couldn't even move! On the other hand, our many layers of clothes kept us warm and protected us from bruising too badly when we fell. Look for light-weight, water-resistant ski clothes, like ski jackets and pants made of Gortex® and silk underwear. Mittens will keep your hands warm but make it hard to maneuver when you need to get a Kleenex® out of your pocket.

4. Don't try to carry a lot of extra stuff with you as you

ski. Sure, you may get hungry, but lunch in a fanny pack may be completely squashed by the time you decide to eat it. Basics for us were tissues, lip balm, and mad money for when we were hungry.

Consider Alternatives: If you are brave enough to choose a ski date as your New Sport Date, let us encourage you to stick with it. As one person put it, "Skiing is some skill, lots of instinct, hard work, insanity, and practice, practice, practice!"

If other safer sports like tennis, golf, or one-on-one basketball are more appealing to you, that's fine. Choose a sport you both will enjoy learning. You're in for an adventure and a treat. By the way, we've even made it down a few black slopes!

12 ♥ Snow Golf Date

Our only golf experience was in the middle of the summer in Albuquerque, New Mexico. Dave's Aunt Jo gave us a Golf Date to introduce us to her favorite sport. She even included a lesson with the local pro.

The Idea: We have more of a spirit of adventure than of athletic ability, but we got into it enough to put golfing on our future list of Sports to Pursue Dates. However, I don't know if we will ever be adventurous enough to try winter golf in the snow. Our friends, Bill and Karen, say it's a great date. Here's their report.

Take Life at a Snow Pace: "Every year we take the time to set goals for the new year and to reflect on our past year together. One January, we hired a sitter to spend the night with our toddler and we took off for an overnight at a local park lodge. It was a beautiful atmosphere. There were few people around as it is basically a summer resort. Our room overlooked a frozen lake and snow-covered golf course.

"That evening we enjoyed a long dinner by candlelight. The warm, glowing fire in the fireplace added to our pleasure and ability to relax as we talked about our marriage, our goals, our love for each other, and our dreams for our lives.

"The next morning, after a leisurely breakfast, we went out and played a round of winter golf. The whole golf course was ours. We didn't have to wait for a group to finish the next hole. We talked continually, with no interruptions, as we drove around the course in our golf cart looking for our orange golf balls in the white snow. It was truly a date filled with love, and lots of communication."

"Who won?" we asked.

"We didn't really keep score," Bill said, "but we both remember winning!"

If you love risks and like the snow, take Bill and Karen's dating suggestion. It's a round of golf you both can win!

13 ♥ Water Date

The Idea: "The ultimate water date" one couple told us, "is to go sailing in the middle of the winter." But unless you live in the South Seas and have your own little sailboat, this also may be the ultimate in expensive dates. Several other couples we know share their enthusiasm, so we are including this date for the rich, though maybe not-so-famous.

Our friends, together with two other couples, flew to the eastern Caribbean Islands where they chartered a fifty-foot sailing yacht. This was not your standard sailboat. It came complete with a captain, cook, and three cozy staterooms with private baths. For one whole week, they sailed around the Virgin Islands.

Our friends swore this was the ultimate date for the workaholic. Think about a week with no phone calls, no television, no contact with your business, no control over things at home. Your only contact with the outside world is the yacht's radio for emergencies!

Reap the Benefits of Limited Space: We are not great water enthusiasts and have absolutely no experience with sailboats, so we asked, "What did you do for a week on a fifty-foot boat?"

Their faces lit up as they told us how they were forced to relax. They ate gourmet food, helped sail the boat, read, snorkeled, swam, sat around, talked, and laughed with their friends. They also said that the V-shaped berths left them no room not to be intimate!

One note of caution from our friends. It is critical that the other couples you go with are very good friends or this date could backfire. A good economy cruise could provide the same background for togetherness (and the stateroom would be larger).

Consider Alternatives: If you are not in the rich and famous category, don't rule out a Water Date. We'll never forget the time we went whitewater rafting—the only time! Claudia spent all of her energy watching and waiting in fear of the famous Devil Shoals. Once back on land, we decided to leave this date for those braver than us.

We hear canoeing can be fun and relaxing. Maybe you like to swim or water ski. Actually the Water Date that sounds the most interesting to us is a Jacuzzi in a nice hotel. Whatever Water Date you choose, just taking the initiative will make a splash with your mate!

14 ♥ Dancing Lessons Date

The Idea: Last Christmas we finally did it. We splurged and bought a new stereo system. For years we used hand-me-down stereo equipment from our three sons. We've had so much fun listening to our old records and tapes, we wonder why we didn't do this sooner. Talk about musical memories—we've got them! Some of our records go way back to our college days and times of dancing cheek-to-cheek. (We were in the era of the Twist.)

Holidays often bring out the sillies in us and last Christmas was no exception. We began to show our family how our generation danced. We also showed ourselves that we could benefit from a Dancing Lessons Date.

Take the First Step: Call Your Local Studio:

Sounds great, but how do we start? Our friend, Michele, suggested calling the local dance studios and asking if they had any specials. The studios also usually know if there are any upcoming free dances or charity balls.

"If you attend a charity ball, you may even be able to deduct at least part of the cost of the tickets from your taxes," Michele told us.

One hotel in our city hosts a free monthly tea dance with Swing music. Occasionally, local dance studios offer drawings. If you are as lucky as Michele, you also may win a free one-hour dance lesson.

Shape Up by Square Dancing: Other friends of ours love to square dance. But let us warn you, we recently went to a square dance and were completely exhausted after a couple of hours. Well after all, it serves us right. This is a Getting in Shape Date! What more can we say?

15 ♥ Workout Date

The Idea: It started with a back injury but led to a fun date. Would you believe that in our late forties we began working out in a fitness gym? Our adult children had a hard time believing their mom was actually pumping iron. But she was, and she has continued her routine for the last two years.

Our Workout Dates actually started a couple of years ago when Claudia injured her back and required several months of therapy. Part of her therapy program was to work out with light weights and do numerous exercises. Not only did this benefit her back, it helped her general physical condition so much that Dave decided (under duress) to join her.

Having lived on the cutting edge of stress and overload for so long, it seemed strange to take the time to work out together. We told ourselves we were doing this for Claudia's back and for our health. But we discovered we were also doing it for fun.

Talk to Your Physician: You can approach a Workout Date several ways. Before you begin working out, however, check out any physical fitness program with your family doctor. Let him or her guide you in what is sensible and healthy for you.

Find a Program within Your Budget: As
you begin, consider your budget and what you can invest
in fitness training. There are many health clubs, aerobic
programs, and fitness centers. We go to a therapy center
for those who have been previously injured. Our strength
trainer, Ed, guides us in what is safe and beneficial for us.
Neither of us is into muscle building; we just want to stay
healthy and have fun in the process.

Work Out with Videos: Don't overlook workout
videos. One couple we know who lives in Germany thinks
these videos are great. The American workout videos add
a touch of home to their life.

A word of caution: This is not a competitive date! Don't
try to outdo each other. Relax, have fun, and enjoy the
fringe benefits of more energy and vigor. You may even
discover being in shape will enhance your other dates—
particularly, the romantic ones! (That's the next part of
this book.)

Romantic Dates

16 ♥ Honeymoon Memory Date

The Idea: Many people tell us that second honeymoons are better than first ones. We tend to agree. Take a few minutes and think back to your own wedding night and honeymoon. If you are like us, you can probably laugh about it now.

We got married in the middle of our college years, during the Cuban Missile Crisis. We thought the Soviets were going to blow up the world before we had a chance to live together. So in two months with slight apprehension at our hurry but mostly with their blessings, our families helped us plan and pull off a lovely church wedding. We just didn't get around to planning our honeymoon!

Back on the Hook: We have always been the spontaneous types. Apart from reservations the first night, we were definitely ad-libbing it with our honeymoon plans. So years later, when others suggested we recreate our honeymoon, we told them, "We're not sure we really want to." Besides, the motel in Gainesville, Georgia, where we spent our wedding night had been torn down long ago. We thought we were off the hook on this date—that is, until Claudia's mom was put in the hospital in Gainesville and we went to see her.

We found ourselves back in the same town at approximately the same time of year as when we were there on our wedding night thirty years ago. When we were not at the hospital, we were working on this book. So naturally, we began to talk about our own honeymoon. As we talked, we realized that the motel where we were staying was located at about the same place where our honeymoon motel had been.

At breakfast that morning, over who knows how many cups of coffee, we reminisced and realized how far we had come in thirty years of marriage. In some small way, we did go back in history. You can do the same. Here are some tips.

Create Your Own Honeymoon:

1. Have a Memory Date to talk once again about your honeymoon. See how far you have come in the months, years, and maybe even decades since your wedding night.

2. Actually go back and recreate (or improve on) your honeymoon.

3. Plan a completely new and updated honeymoon. We like this suggestion and have decided we would rather go to Austria than Gainesville, Georgia!

4. Be thankful for all you've learned in your marriage and for all the ways you've grown closer to each other.

17 ♥ Three Wishes Date

The Idea: Yes, our friend actually met her husband at the door one evening in a tutu complete with wings, quiver, and three arrows with hearts. "Tonight is your night!" she told him. "I'm your Fairy Godmother and I will grant you three wishes!"

Our friend was quite sketchy about what happened next, but the giggle and silly look on her face told us it was a fun, romantic date. While not asking specific details, we did gather some practical suggestions in case you feel like turning into a Fairy Godmother or Fairy Godfather.

Heed the Warnings: It's best to make this a surprise date. But you've also got to be in the mood for this one. Announcing the day or morning before the date that you're set to be the wish-granting fairy may set both of you up for a letdown. Expectations may build too much. Or your day may get out of hand and be one of those awful days that if you were a fairy, you'd want to make yourself disappear—much less grant wishes!

One more caution: Some may find that granting three unqualified wishes is a little too threatening. What if a mate asks you to do something you don't want to do? If you are worried about this, you can ask your mate for five wishes; then choose the three you feel comfortable granting. You may be able to relax more this way and enjoy bringing pleasure to your mate.

Make a List of Your Wishes: Here are a few wish suggestions:

- Thirty-minute back rub
- Foot massage and pedicure
- Bath—gently bathe your mate, as if you were bathing a baby
- Shower for two—take a shower together and wash each other's hair.

Our list ends here, but this can be the beginning of your own brand of creativity. This is one date the fairy godparent may enjoy as much as the lucky subject. At any rate it should add some sparkle to your love life.

18 ❤ Kidnap Date

The Idea: Are you looking for a way to rekindle the flame of romance in your relationship? Why not do the unexpected?

Claudia will never forget the day Dave came in with three red roses and announced they were leaving in thirty minutes. Off he whisked her to a little hotel in the Vienna Woods. (We were living in Vienna at that time.) After Claudia called and confirmed that there really was a sitter with our three boys, she relaxed. Together, we enjoyed a wonderfully intimate two days and two nights alone.

Romance can be alive and well in your marriage too. Why not kidnap your mate? The element of surprise in the Kidnap Date recreates that feeling you had when you dated before you married. Others have pulled it off. Listen to one wife's account.

Plan to Take Time Apart: "We've found in our sixteen years of marriage, our weekend getaways keep the spark alive and add spice to our life. Plus there's something about getting away together that creates an atmosphere of relaxation. Uninterrupted time to focus on one another, to talk and laugh and love each other, are like marital vitamins.

"We regularly get away one weekend every other month. We swap kids with another family so every other month we have their children for a weekend. For us, it's really worth it. So when I decided to surprise my husband, baby-sitting was already taken care of.

"I contacted my husband's business and, unknown to him, arranged for him to leave early on Friday afternoon. Others in his office cooperated and covered his appointments and other commitments. I then worked out the children's after-school schedule and rides to the home where they were spending the weekend.

"Friday finally arrived. I felt like a kid again. I packed the car with our clothes, food munchies, favorite music, candles, bubble bath—you get the picture! I then picked up my husband at work, blindfolded him, and led him to the car—the passenger side. I instructed him to lie back and relax while I drove to our mountain hideaway about forty-five minutes away. I previously reserved a room with our own fireplace and jacuzzi. Let the fun begin!"

Make the Most of the Unexpected: "When
we arrived, my husband was so excited about our romantic weekend away he couldn't unload the car fast enough. Now as much as I'd like to leave the rest of our romantic rendezvous to your imagination, I have to be honest and tell you what happened next.

"As he bent over to set our luggage down, his back went into spasm. Yes, we did spend the weekend in bed, but it wasn't quite as romantic as what we had in mind. However, the weekend is still one of our favorite memories. We had hours and hours just to talk. There were no interruptions. He couldn't move, so there was no place to go.

"We reaffirmed our commitment to one another. How

does it go? 'In sickness and in health . . .' We can now add, 'With healthy backs and with hurting backs!' "

Laugh at the Memories—Good and Bad:
The Arps also have had our disappointments—like the time we were staying at a romantic country inn and got locked out. We ended up spending the night in our VW camper! But let us encourage you to keep planning and keep surprising each other. Even the times things don't work out as planned, you're left with memories you can laugh about someday. So go on. Take the chance. Kidnap your mate. He or she will be a happy hostage!

19 ♥ At-Home Romance Date

The Idea: "Believe it or not," a mother of two young children told us, "one of our favorite romantic dates is at home."

"You've got to be kidding," we said in unison. But she meant it. "How do you pull it off?" we asked. Here's her secret.

Plan Ahead: "First, I find out what time my husband expects to arrive home. Then I plan ahead, feed the kids, and get them ready for bed.

"I usually have music playing, candles lit, and dinner warming in the oven by the time he walks in the door. I ask him to put the kids to bed while I'm in the bathroom running a hot bubble bath and lighting candles around the tub.

"After he tucks the children in bed and says goodnight, I lead him to the bedroom, undress him, then bathe him. Then, I tell him to soak and relax while I set out dinner on a picnic blanket in front of the fireplace in a candlelit room.

"When he comes downstairs in his robe, the phone is either off the hook or on first ring on our answering machine. The rest is optional!"

Coach the Children: "But what about the children?" we asked.

"The children have been coached all day that tonight is special for Daddy and Mommy," she said. "I tell them it is very important that they do their part by obeying rules and staying in bed."

Consider Alternatives: Now, we must make a date disclaimer. When our sons were little, no way would we have trusted those three to stay in bed. However, if your kids are more obedient than ours were and you're a brave and adventurous soul, you can go ahead and give this At-Home Romance Date a try. But if, like us, you're not so brave, farm the kids out for the evening. The rest is up to your ingenuity!

20 ♥ Bed and Breakfast Date

The Idea: Our very first Bed and Breakfast Date started with a Christmas present from Joel and Jeanne. They gave us a wonderful Bed and Breakfast guidebook with vivid descriptions of B & B's around the country. Knowing our empty nest was fast approaching, they wanted us to be prepared for a new kind of date. So far each time we have used their gift, we haven't been disappointed.

Interestingly, some of our favorites aren't the elaborate, expensive ones. We like to stay in places that are a little more austere and have lots of history. They are usually cheaper too!

Look for Someplace Unique: That we at least passed something down to the next generation became obvious when Joel and Jeanne described one of their favorite Bed and Breakfast Dates. They went to an old, old hotel in Minnesota called the Anderson House. Its uniqueness? It's the oldest operating hotel in that state, dating back to the 1850s and is still run by the original family (or at least by their descendants).

Joel and Jeanne liked the Dutch European influence in the structure of the building. It wasn't your upscale hotel, but it was unusual and eccentric. For instance, it had seventeen house cats guests could rent for the night. Joel and

Jeanne love cats and have two of their own. So they had fun renting a cat for the evening but admitted they felt unfaithful to their cats, Pete and Sebastian.

We're not sure we would go so far as to rent a cat, but recently, when we were visiting Joel and Jeanne, we left the door to our room cracked one night so Pete and Sebastian could visit us. We hear that petting a cat lowers your blood pressure. Perhaps that's what makes the Anderson House such a relaxing place to stay.

Check This List Before You Go: If we have whetted your appetite for a Bed and Breakfast Date, consider the following few tips.

1. Make reservations well in advance. We can still hear the owner of one B & B laughing. We called for reservations the day of our trip and discovered they book their rooms years in advance. That's unusual, but it is wise to book your accommodations several weeks or months in advance.

2. Ask about their smoking or non-smoking policy. Most B & B's are small and smoke may carry throughout the house. Claudia has an allergy to smoke. Once we stayed in a quaint, old house but both of the owners and all the other guests smoked. It was not one of our most pleasant experiences.

3. Check the pet policy. Some allow pets while others don't. This may affect you even if you don't have pets. We'll long remember one B & B experience. It was not unlike the Anderson Cat Hotel, but dogs were the pet of choice. The owner had two dogs and the other guest had two dogs about the size of Shetland ponies. There almost wasn't room for us and the rest of the guests.

4. Visit bed and breakfasts with a spirit of adventure.

You will find that no two are the same. On your Book Date (see page 17) you may want to check out books on bed and breakfasts and country inns. The book we received as a Christmas present has been fun to use and is revised each year. The title is *Country Inns and Back Roads, North America* by Norman T. Simpson. It is part of the Berkshire Traveller Series and is published annually by Harper and Row, New York. Another book of interest is *Bed and Breakfast U.S.A. 1992* by Betty Rundback (Plume 1992). In addition AAA has given us good travel information. Local travel agencies also may be helpful.

Most helpful of all is the chance to get away together and explore. Choose your own style—from country inns to seaside or mountain lodges, mansions, farm houses, or ranches. Who knows what adventures lurk just ahead? You may even end up renting your very own cat!

21 ♥ Swinging in the Jungle Date

The Idea: Do you harbor a secret desire to go on an African safari? Or maybe you dream about a vacation for two on a deserted island, but your budget is a better fit with the dollar theater and popcorn. If so, you may be a candidate for a Swinging in the Jungle Date. Our friends say it's more fun than a barrel of monkeys. Here's how the wife describes this special date.

"The night before our first jungle date we sat and stared at our depleted checkbook. The funds weren't there for a major vacation that summer, and we had just made a commitment to let credit cards lie and collect dust instead of interest. Seeing my husband's disappointment motivated me to come up with an 'at home' fun getaway date. Thus the origination of our Swinging in the Jungle Date."

Bring Him/Her Home with a Mysterious Invitation:
"First I called my husband and left a message on his voice mail something like, 'Honey, I'm so glad you chose me as your mate. . . . We may not be able to afford an African safari, but let's swing in the jungle tonight. See you later!'"

Dress for the Jungle:
"When he arrived home, I met him at the door in Me Jane attire. (I wore an aerobic workout outfit and leotard skirt.) I then led Tarzan to a

picnic dinner set up in our backyard tree house. If you don't have a tree house, improvise with a picnic table and blanket. If the weather is inclement, consider the screened porch. If it's cold, set up your jungle in the den or in front of the fireplace. Add plants all around to resemble a jungle."

Keep the Fare Simple: "I tried to be creative with the picnic food and to carry out the jungle theme with bananas, coconuts, berries, pineapples, nuts, and mangoes. Candles added to the atmosphere, but later we blew them out and watched the moon and stars appear. It wasn't quite like Africa, but it sure beat leftovers!

"The next summer we were able to take a vacation, but tucked in our memory bank of fun experiences is our night at home swinging in the jungle!"

22 ♥ Clue Date

Surprises run in our family. When Jarrett and Laurie were dating, Jarrett surprised Laurie by chartering a small plane and flying them around the Chicago skyline. Laurie had no idea where they were going. The original plan was to land at an airport in downtown Chicago, go out for dinner and to the theater, and then take a limousine back to the college campus. When Jarrett found out how much all of that would cost, this romantic dude realized that even five-star dates have their limit and he stuck with just the plane ride!

The Idea: If your mate likes surprises and enjoys not knowing where you are going or what you are doing, why not have a Clue Date? Give your mate clues—perhaps in poetry or jingles if you are poetic or wish to be—for each part of your special date. Try the following.

Leave a Creative Trail of Clues:

Clue One—This clue might include the invitation and suggestion of attire for the date. You might say something like:

How about a date Friday night at eight?
It will be far from normal, so please dress formal!

Clue Two—Give a hint of where you are going. If you are going to an outdoor concert you could give this clue:

> Music is fun and calms the soul,
> But take a coat because it may be cold!

Another place you might consider going to is a favorite restaurant. If your budget is tight, go out for dessert or a cup of coffee or tea. Plays, lectures, and movies are also great places to go on Clue Dates. Dave once planned a great Clue Date to the dollar theater!

Clue Three—To top off a romantic evening, you may whisk your mate off to a motel with a jacuzzi or hot tub, or take your mate home and pretend your bathroom is a spa. For this part of the evening, you could give this clue:

> Rub a dub dub, two lovers in a tub!

We suggest following your "water adventure" with an extensive back rub by candlelight. For a warm romantic feeling, use lotion you've warmed in the microwave.

Consider Alternatives: Another type of Clue Date your mate will appreciate is a special delivery letter complete with clues, inviting him or her for a date. (Actually, now it is called Priority Mail or Overnight Express Mail.) An inexpensive way to have a letter personally delivered is to send it UPS. If you want to include flowers with your invitation you can use FTD florists. In your invitation include the time to be ready for your date and what to wear. For example, you may suggest wearing warm-ups and surprise your mate with a romantic walk at night!

Surprise dates can be elaborate or simple, expensive or

cheap, long or short. They can add fun, excitement, and adventure to your dating life. They are great rut-removers and can be the spark to add romance to your marriage. Give it a try. You may be surprised at the results!

Do It Together Dates

23 ♥ Home Improvement Date

The Idea: From time to time we have dreamed of restoring an old house. Our dreams, however, always include the wherewithal to do it. If we had to do the work ourselves, it would be a nightmare. We're not that handy, but Joel and Jeanne are.

This time the genes skipped a generation. We realized this when Joel and Jeanne bought their first house, an old English Tudor built in 1931. We were able to combine a speaking engagement with a visit with them in their "new" old home, so we offered to be their slaves for several days.

It was actually fun to scrub, clean, hang wallpaper, unpack boxes, and be their helpers. It also brought back memories of our eleven moves, which have spanned several continents, as well as memories of all of our Home Improvement Dates! To be honest, we didn't really call them dates at the time, but we do have some happy memories.

Wallpapering Dates are probably our favorite. It may take two to tango, but for us it definitely takes two to wallpaper. We have our system down. Dave applies the paste. Claudia hangs the paper. And we both feel proud when it stays on the wall!

Beware of the Hazards: Once, when we were living in Vienna, we wallpapered our whole apartment. Our bedroom was the last room, and we were running low on wallpaper paste. No problem, we simply thinned it. That was in the summer. That winter when the heat came on and the walls adjusted to the change of climate, our wallpaper decided to adjust too. In the middle of one night, we heard a rustling sound. We turned on the light just in time to see our wallpaper peeling off the wall in large strips. The next day we had another Wallpaper Date to rehang it!

Make a To-Do List: What projects would you love to get accomplished around your house? Why not make a list? Then check your latent talents and resources. Some couples love to paint together. We know one couple who painted the outside of their house. Maybe you really want to clean out and organize the basement. Tackle it together.

Look for Ways to Learn the Skills You Lack: If you're worried about your home improvement skills, or lack thereof, take heart. Joel and Jeanne are multitalented. They can do anything from repairing cracks in plaster walls to hanging blinds and wallpaper. When we asked them how they learned to hang wallpaper (we learned the hit or miss method), we were surprised to find out they had learned from watching a video. Clever!

You may want to check your local video store and see if there is a video giving instructions for what you want to do. Also, some stores offer how-to classes and have videos for loan. This could even be another date—to watch home improvement videos and choose your home improvement project. You may even decide to take a class. Not only will your home be improved, but you may enjoy the process.

24 ♥ Study Date

The Idea: We've decided that learning keeps you young and keeps your life from stagnating. So our next Do It Together Date suggestion is to take a class together.

Adult educational opportunities abound, especially if you live in a town with a college or university. You can find classes offered in everything from aerobics to art appreciation. Your local YMCA/YWCA also offers many kinds of classes.

Consider the Possibilities: Consider taking classes or lessons in one of the following areas:

- Music appreciation
- Art history
- Ceramics and pottery
- Music (One couple we know recently learned to play the guitar.)
- Art
- Financial management
- Bible/Religion/Theology
- Voice
- Aerobics
- Foreign language

Add the subjects or skills you've dreamed of learning about to our list, and choose something you'd like to learn together. We chose the last one, but it was under duress and out of need.

Consider the Benefits: We were living in Vienna and were doing okay with our German in day-to-day living. But to be really effective, we needed to be able to lead marriage workshops in the German language. This required a big (actually a huge) step up from our present level of speaking German, so we decided to take a class together.

The class only lasted a couple of months, so we weren't overwhelmed. We had a goal we could manage; we knew there was a starting point and a finish line.

For some reason language learning is easier for Dave (maybe because he lived in Austria as a young boy), so Claudia needed all the encouragement Dave could give her. We found it was fun to study together—especially after class in a small Viennese coffee shop.

There were other benefits. We met interesting people in the class, including a high government official from France and an American girl with whom we still keep up. It was a rewarding experience for us, so it's easy to suggest that you choose your own field of study and grow together with your mate.

25 ♥ Remember When Date

The Idea: Face it. Some things just have to get done. Why not turn some of the mundane chores of life into a fun date. Most any job is more enjoyable when you tackle it together. It helps, too, if you can make a game out of it. We suggest you try remembering when.

Back in ages past—before you were married—remember how much you looked forward to doing routine chores together? We remember finding our little terrace apartment (now it would be considered a basement ghetto) and how much we looked forward to living there together. As we stood in the small kitchen, we couldn't wait to share the joy of washing and drying our very own dishes. Even making up our bed and cleaning the bathroom sounded romantic then. My, how things change!

If things have changed at your house too, if you're under the pile and need a united front to get back on top, consider turning your chores into a Remember When Date. As you do routine chores together, remember when you dreamed about doing these things together—before you were married.

Take a Refreshing Step Back in Time: Recently, we were in Atlanta, Georgia, and decided to see if we could still remember how to get to our first apartment. We actually did find it and sat in our car and remembered.

"Remember when we spent a whole day picking out our china and crystal and registering at the local department store?" If you haven't used your good dishes for a long time, perhaps you need to plan a special At Home Dinner-for-Two Date.

"Remember when we received our first wedding gift?" As you dust knickknacks, try to remember who gave them to you or on what special occasion you acquired them.

"Remember when we used to go to the laundromat to wash our clothes?" When our clothes were all dirty, we would feel the urge to spend a weekend with Claudia's parents. They had a great washer and dryer and lived only eighty miles away!

Consider Alternatives: A variation of the Remember When Date is to grocery shop together. As you go up and down the aisles, remember the first times you grocery shopped together. We remember having an argument over angel food cake. Dave picked up an angel food cake mix. Claudia was insulted that he thought she couldn't make one from scratch. (Now, we simply buy one from the bakery.) Notice items you used to purchase that you no longer need. We zip right by the baby food section, animal crackers, and Gatorade!

Remember in Silence: If you prefer working together in silence, you may want to make a mental list of your own Remember Whens. Then, at the end of the day, share a pizza and your lists with each other. Just remembering when working together was such fun may encourage you to tackle your present to-do list as a team.

26 ♥ Marriage Enrichment Workshop Date

The Idea: If you have never participated in a Marriage Enrichment event, we highly recommend this date. Your own marriage relationship will be enriched as you interact with other couples who are committed to making their marriage grow.

Keep Your Marriage Alive: In 1973, on their fortieth wedding anniversary, the Maces founded the Association of Couples in Marriage Enrichment (ACME), an international network of persons working for better marriages. The Association focuses on problem prevention, growth, and potential. Couples learn to communicate effectively, to deal creatively with anger, to negotiate differences, and to express appreciation. We became involved in ACME in 1983 when we attended an ACME Leaders Training Workshop that David and Vera Mace led. The group was small, so we had plenty of time to talk with the other couples and with the Maces.

We were intrigued by this couple who were in their late seventies and still had a vibrant, loving, and alive marriage, a commitment they had kept for fifty years. We returned for the advanced training also led by the Maces.

And over the years they have had substantial input into our lives.

David passed away in 1990, but we continue to stay in touch with Vera. Now in her nineties, she is still actively encouraging couples. She even gave suggestions for our last book, *The Marriage Track.*

Seminar Suggestions: We joyfully endorse and commend ACME to you. Through weekend retreats, local marriage growth groups and conferences, you'll have the opportunity to continue to enrich your marriage relationship. ACME activities are for couples of all ages and at all stages of marriage. Their popular Newlywed Program helps couples learn to relate positively during the critical period soon after marriage. For further information contact:

ACME
P.O. Box 10596
Winston-Salem, NC 27108

We also recommend the Minirth-Meier Clinic's Passages of Marriage Conference as well as our own Marriage Alive Workshop. The Passages of Marriage Conference is for large groups, while the Marriage Alive Workshop is a resource for smaller groups. For information about how your church or organization can host a Marriage Alive Workshop contact:

Marriage Alive International
P.O. Box 90303

Knoxville, TN 37990
Telephone: 615-691-8505

For information about Passages of Marriage Conferences you can call toll-free 1-800-229-3000.

27 ♥ Host a Dinner Party Date

The Idea: We don't have the gourmet cooking ability our sons and daughters-in-law have, but a couple of Dinner Party Dates we've pulled off stand out in our memory bank as super fun.

Give a Friend from Another Country a Taste of American Tradition:
The first was a Valentine dinner party we gave for our German friends when we were living in Germany. Valentine's Day originated in Italy, but we have adopted the holiday into our American tradition. Valentine's isn't celebrated in Germany, so we decided to give our German friends a little taste of America.

What made this dinner party so much fun was an offer by our good friends, Clark and Ann, to be our servants for the evening. Their German was better than ours which helped the after-dinner conversation. Our friends especially liked the cherry pie and our stories about George Washington and the cherry tree. (We included a little American history in our celebration.)

Invite a Special Guest or Speaker:
Our other favorite Dinner Party Date was in Vienna when we hosted a dinner in our home for our Austrian friends. Our guests of honor were Stan and Margie Smith. Tennis fans

will immediately recognize Stan Smith as one of the world's tennis greats. He was in Vienna playing in a tennis tournament and graciously agreed to come share about his tennis and personal life with our friends. We met the Smiths through mutual friends, also living in Vienna. They not only co-hosted the dinner with us, they provided a caterer to do all the work! Now you know why it was such a favorite date.

Plan a Planning Date: If funds for catering aren't there and you don't have friends willing to be your servants, don't discard this date suggestion. Our friends, Janie and John, assure us it's fun to pull it off on your own. Janie tells us about it.

"Don't let the idea of hosting a dinner party scare you. It may be more fun than work—especially if you tackle it as an extended date with your mate. We've had so much fun that we've organized a monthly gourmet club with two other couples and alternate among our three homes. John has even discovered a new hobby—cooking! This makes it all the more enjoyable. We now have a whole string of dates for each dinner party.

"Our initial date is to plan the menu. We enjoy thumbing through gourmet magazines and special occasion cookbooks. John usually chooses the entree since he cooks that part of the meal. Together we decide what side dishes and appetizers complement the meal. I like to choose the dessert for the evening. After planning the menu, we compile our shopping list.

"On our second date we grocery shop together. We like to go to a local grocery store that serves samples and gourmet coffee to their shoppers.

"The next evening, we decide how the meal will be served. For example, will it be formal or informal, inside or outside? Will we use our good china or everyday dishes?

"The night before our dinner party is the Food Preparation Date. Whatever can be done ahead of time we do, from chopping vegetables to making sauces to baking bread. It helps to put on our favorite CD or cassette tape. This is also the time we give the house a once over—at least the areas we are using for our dinner party.

"One of the ideas behind our Pre-dinner Party Dates is to be prepared so we can enjoy the evening with our guests. We try to be dressed and completely prepared at least an hour before our guests arrive. That gives us time for a last-minute check and then time to sit down, relax, and have hors d'oeuvres together. When our doorbell rings, we are ready to greet our guests with a warm welcome and to give them an evening of fun, good food, and relaxation."

One more tip from Janie and John is to keep tabs of the grocery bill. Because their gourmet club is a regular monthly affair, the three couples divide the cost of each meal. They say it's much cheaper than going out to a nice restaurant. The only down side is you do have to wash the dishes and clean up, but it still sounds like a fun date to us. But the atmosphere is more relaxing because there are no time limitations and are no other customers waiting for your table.

Consider Alternatives: Here's one final tip. If you are like us and your time and creativity are limited, but you still want to host a dinner party, we suggest let-ting Julia Child help you. *The Julia Child's Menu Cookbook* (Wings Books, 1991) contains 26 menus for cooking for company. It will help you make your Dinner Party Date as delightful for you as it is for your guest!

28 ♥ Marriage History Date

The Idea: If you've been married longer than twenty-four hours, you have a marriage history. If you've been married longer than twenty-four years, you may have forgotten your marriage history! For the latter, this date will help you remember. For the former, it will help you not forget your good times together.

What is a Marriage History Date? It's anything you choose to do to catalog your good times together from writing a marriage journal to producing your own video.

Over the years we've had several dates that helped us catalog our marriage history. We love pictures, so we have trays of slides and boxes of snapshots. Before the days of video cameras, we put together our own family slide shows, complete with a soundtrack. Today, we use them as a fun way to relive some of our marriage history.

Get Out the Slides: One slide show Claudia and our sons made as a surprise for Dave is especially meaningful to us. It starts with our dating days and follows with the birth and history of each son. We knew our sons were serious about a girl when they pulled out this slide show and revealed what our family was really like. It's only been shown to two girls and both are now our daughters-in-law!

Make a Scrapbook: One couple we know have a date each year to make a scrapbook of their marriage history for the past twelve months. They include photos, napkins, hotel receipts—whatever conjures up happy memories.

Produce a Video: Another pair have a standing video date. Every year they plan a special date for their anniversary. Their date includes a candlelight dinner and their video camera. Over dinner they discuss the major events of the last year and jot down their thoughts. After dinner, with their video camera on a tripod, they record their own marriage history for the past twelve months.

Our friends are the organized type. They have edited all their anniversary videos together on one tape. Do they really watch them? we asked. Here's what they said.

"Yes we do, and it's bunches of fun. It's amazing to see the difference in our lives from year to year. Not only do we change in our appearance (a few extra pounds here and there, different hair styles, different clothes), but even more interesting is to see how we have matured and grown closer to each other.

"We've been working on our marriage for eleven years. With so much history behind us, we're going to keep at it. For us marriage is a lifetime commitment. We could never split—we only have one video!"

Include the Essentials: If you want to video your own marriage history, here are some suggestions of things to include:

- Year, month, and day and what you are celebrating (anniversary, birthday, promotion, or a move to a new location)
- Major happenings of the last year (If you are just starting this dating tradition, you may want to include a brief summary of your life together, including where you have lived and special things you have done together.)
- Humorous happenings
- Things you are looking forward to this next year

Whether you collect photos or slides, make videos or write marriage history books, you'll enjoy this date for years to come. Think of all the good times together you'll someday be able to remember!

29 ♥ Home Depot Date

The Idea: Where was Home Depot when we needed it years ago?

As we have already indicated, we're not too handy around the house, but establishments like Home Depot, which sell hardware and home decorations, are making it easier for people like us. We appreciate the good advice and tips the staff give happily and at no extra cost. Claudia was a little leery when she ordered dark blue paint for a bedroom and the salesperson who mixed the paint tried to convince her the room would look like a dungeon. This time he was wrong, but usually we've gotten excellent tips.

We became well-acquainted with Home Depot the year we did some empty-nest remodeling. But we never considered going there as a date until our friend Pamela told us that her favorite date with her husband, Evans, was to go to Home Depot.

Try Out Pamela's Idea: "You mean," we questioned, "you actually plan a date to go to Home Depot when you don't need anything?" Pamela convinced us the trip could be a relaxing, inexpensive, and fun evening.

"Recently Evans and I bought our first house. It's a fixer-upper, and for us it's a long term project. We do projects as we have the time and money. Since right now both seem evasive, we enjoy dreaming and getting ideas for future improvements. For us, this makes for a great date."

It took us awhile to adjust our thinking and put Home Depot and dating in the same category. We asked Pamela for more details. "If you're not there out of the need to fix something specific, what do you do?"

She assured us it is fun just to go up and down the aisles and talk about what you would like to do in the future. "Also," she added, "you can get great ideas from their kitchen and bath displays."

We began to see her point, so we tried her date suggestion. Claudia loved the garden windows and knows just the place for one in our kitchen. Dave was fascinated with the mirror tiles.

Pamela suggested writing down your ideas and putting them in a file for future reference. She also suggested topping off your date with eating dinner out or catching a movie.

If you pursue this date, here's a tip from the Arps. Watch out for impulse buying. Dave had to return the mirror tiles!

30 ♥ Marriage Checkup Date

The Idea: We suggest that every couple, no matter how long they've been married, have an annual Marriage Checkup Date. It can be a growing and enriching experience.

Get What You Need to Get Started: All that is needed for this date are two pens, some paper, and time alone together. Plan for a couple of hours of peace and quiet. Better still, if possible, go away overnight. This may be a great date to combine with a Bed and Breakfast Date.

Start by answering the following questions. You may want to write out your answers separately and then discuss them together.

1. What do I like most about my mate? (For instance Claudia would have to say Dave's easygoing personality and listening ear.) The thing I like most about my mate is:

_____.

2. What was the best thing that happened to us as a couple in the last twelve months? (Dave might say, the time we spent alone together in New England and setting fresh goals for our marriage.) The best thing that happened to us as a couple in the last twelve months was: _

_____.

3. If my mate had the power to change one thing about me, what do I think he or she would change? (Claudia is

sure Dave would say that she should be neater—
especially with the horizontal files on her desk.) The one
thing I think my mate would like to change about me is:

_____.

4. Write down five things you'd like to do together with
your mate in the next year. (Dave's list might include getting our home office organized and getting away for a
week alone in the mountains or at the beach. Claudia
would be sure to include writing a new book and continuing to exercise together.) Five things I would like to do in
this next year with my mate are:

1. _____.
2. _____.
3. _____.
4. _____.
5. _____.

Set Goals Together: As you enjoy reflecting on
the past twelve months of your marriage, set goals for the
next twelve months. Combine your list of things you
would like to do together and set priorities. Pick a time
and place to do your number-one priority. During the next
twelve months, work your way through as much of your
combined list as possible. This may be one annual
checkup you'll look forward to!

Cheap and Easy Dates

31 ♥ Game Date

Have you noticed a subtle shift in our culture? From our observations, relationships seem to be in and the extravagance of the 1980s on the way out. In the 1990s there seems to be a desire to get back to the basics, to slow down the pace, and to return to a simpler life-style.

The Idea: Not long ago when we were in Wisconsin, friends took us to a quaint shopping mall for breakfast. As we were leaving, a man drove up in his horse and buggy. *My,* we thought, *they even have tourist rides here, but who would want to ride a horse and buggy in the snow?*

As we watched the man tie his horse to a pole in the parking lot and then place a blanket on the back of his horse, we began to realize he wasn't there to drive tourists around. We were in Amish country and he was for real. We assume his buggy didn't come with heating or air conditioning. While we want a simpler life, we don't want to go that far! But we are willing to start the process with a Cheap and Easy Game Date.

Choose Your Favorite Game: Actually this is a fun date from our past. It was just what we could afford when our boys were little and our finances were limited. We needed something cheap, but also easy, so we began our Backgammon Dates. After we got our tribe in bed, we would pull out our backgammon game and go at it. We don't remember who usually won, but we do remember it as being fun and definitely cheap!

One couple we know enjoys popping popcorn and putting together jigsaw puzzles. That's not for us. Claudia would love it, but Dave thinks puzzles are a total waste of time. One of our worst arguments was over putting together a puzzle. For Claudia, it was relaxing and she wanted Dave to help her. He found it totally frustrating and definitely not relaxing. He still doesn't understand why any sane person would spend hours and hours hunting for little pieces that don't fit. We finally compromised by only putting puzzles together on vacations and one at Christmas.

Plan a Shop Date: What is your favorite game? Checkers? Chess? Double Solitaire? Scrabble? If you're not sure, why not plan a date to shop for a game. It may be an investment in many fun future dates.

Ask your friends what their favorite games are. You may get some good suggestions. We never got into video games, but others seem to enjoy them. One couple even created their own computer game. When we asked about it, they turned red and said it was too personal.

If your nest is empty, look through all those shelves filled with things your kids left behind in their rooms and see what games you can find. I bet we could even find our Backgammon set. Who knows? We may revive this cheap and easy date, but you can be sure we will let the boxes of puzzles continue to collect dust.

32 ♥ Music Date

The Idea: One thing we loved about living in Vienna was the beautiful music. And we were amazed that much of it was free! Our favorite Music Date was going to Stadt Park, a lovely park near the Opera in downtown Vienna. Not only was the music gratis, but it was accompanied by professional dancers performing Viennese waltzes.

Often as we walked through the streets of Vienna or Salzburg, musicians performed for anyone who would stop and listen. In Austria free music abounded, but once we moved back to the States, we had to look for it. And we finally did. So can you.

Look for Community Concerts: Here in our
hometown of Knoxville, there are free concerts from time to time at the World's Fair Park. Occasionally, the City Symphony gives free performances. Other concerts are quite inexpensive. Last Christmas, tickets for the *Messiah* were only five dollars each.

Keep your ears and eyes open for new artists. You may be among the first to hear a future great. We went to an inexpensive concert one evening, where we heard Garth Brooks perform, so when he first made it, we were among the few who actually knew who he was.

You can also check your local newspaper for free music recitals. If you live near a college or university with a good music department, check with them for a listing of free or inexpensive recitals and concerts. Another source of free concerts is local churches. Our church has several concerts with a full orchestra each year.

Watch for Special Weekend Events: Local eating establishments may offer live music, especially on the weekends. A cheap and easy tip from one couple is to order only appetizers or desserts. You can enjoy the entertainment, but your bill won't be exorbitant.

Make a Date to Shop for Music: For a Music Date with future benefits, make a date to shop for a new CD or audio music tape. If your budget is really tight, go to a bookstore that sells used CDs and tapes. (You may have to use willpower to buy just one, but remember this is a cheap date.) Then return home, make a pot of tea, cuddle on the couch, and let the music fill the room. You never know where this date may lead!

33 ♥ Window Shopping Date

The Idea: Window Shopping Dates are really inexpensive, especially if you go when the stores are closed! And they are even more fun if the one who likes window shopping the least initiates it. Or so says our friend Karen.

Make It a Surprise: "We have a home-based business. With two small children, things can get pretty hectic and tense. We don't have regular help in our office, but on this particular day my husband, Bill, had scheduled someone to help him. They worked diligently in the office all morning.

"As I began to prepare lunch for us and our two preschoolers, in walked Bill's helper. 'I'll finish that,' she said. Imagine my surprise when I looked up and saw my husband standing at the door with my coat in hand waiting for me.

"What really excited me was the fact that he had planned (no twisted arm) to take me on my favorite free adventure date—window shopping! Also, he had figured out the baby-sitting (our office helper), and I didn't have to spend hours getting ready. All I had to do was put on my coat!

"First, we went to the dollar matinee at our local theater. Then, over lunch we talked and talked. Next, we hit the shopping malls to window shop. It was inexpensive because we didn't go in any of the stores. We just enjoyed looking."

Dave can empathize with Bill who is not an "inside the store shopper," but he, too, is willing to go window shopping occasionally. For us to make sure this is a cheap and easy date, we go when the stores are closed. We don't always have Bill and Karen's willpower!

Consider the Added Benefit: Here's another twist. As you window shop, pick out all the things you already have that you see in the store windows. Most of us have more than we realize. Be thankful for the abundance of blessings you have and the opportunity to have a cheap and easy date.

34 ♥ Mate Appreciation Date

The Idea: According to a recent survey, the three top things Americans value are faith in God, good health, and family relationships. Surprisingly, material possessions and accumulation of wealth are way down on the list. This tells us that people are looking for ways to enrich their intimate relationships. Yet, we are often still more kind and show more appreciation to perfect strangers than we do toward our mates. We can't remember being rude to a clerk in a store or to a grocery bag person, yet it's so easy to slip and say unkind things to our mate.

To combat that tendency and to enhance your intimacy, we suggest the following Mate Appreciation Date.

Take Time to Prepare Before the Date:
Before your date, take time to answer the following questions.

1. What personal traits are special to you about your mate? (For example, Dave might list Claudia's creativity, endless energy and enthusiasm, and wisdom.) My mate's traits that are special to me are: ___

_____

_____ .

2. What has your mate done lately that you especially like? (When Claudia was trying to meet a criti-

cal writing deadline, Dave surprised her with her favorite take-out Chinese food.) I especially appreciated
it when my mate: _____

_____

_____.

3. What do you particularly enjoy doing together?
(Claudia might list traveling together.) The thing I
enjoy most doing with my mate is: _____

_____

_____.

Why not go to your favorite park or restaurant and
share your list with each other? It takes no money to af-
firm your mate but the benefits are something money
can't buy!

35 ♥ Parade of Homes Date

The Idea: Many cities across the United States have an annual parade of homes that features the latest in home design for the eager viewers and prospective home buyers.

We're not in the market for a new home, but we do have a standing date to go to the Parade of Homes each year. For five bucks, we can visit three different home developments. (We usually make that three dates within the ten days of the Parade of Homes.)

Just Pretend: You can have fun imagining what your life would be like if you lived in the different homes in the parade. One year all of the homes were small starters. We had fun thinking back and fantasizing, "How would we like each house if we were just starting out?"

The year we were helping our own home go through the "change of life"—that time when everything wears out —we got great ideas and leads on who is the best and cheapest at various remodeling tasks. (Warning: This date is initially cheap, but it has the potential of requiring future funding.)

The fantasy turns back into reality when you get the facts sheet provided at most of the homes. This sheet includes information about the house such as the square footage, room dimensions, mortgage information, and estimated monthly payments. After reading these every year, we return home and look around at our modest house, thankful for what we have and for our relatively low house payments.

Watch the Papers: Check out your own area. If you don't have something similar to our Parade of Homes, watch the papers for open houses. It's a great way to pick up new ideas and a fun way to date your mate!

36 ♥ Switch Date

The Idea: This did not start out as a date. It started out as a frustrating drive to church!

Be Willing to Make Fun from Frustration:
Dave couldn't find his billfold with his driver's license, so Claudia had to drive. We must tell you that driving is not her favorite activity. She assumes if we are going somewhere together, Dave will drive.

After church Claudia wasn't quite as irritated, so she opened the car door for Dave and gave him the royal treatment. Instead of driving him home, she took him out for lunch. Of course, she had to pay because he had neither money nor driver's license.

By then, we were really into our roles and for the rest of the day, we played "switch." Claudia even drove Dave back to church that evening. (By the way, he found his billfold. It was with the glasses he had also misplaced.)

Keep It Simple: Years ago, when men typically planned and paid for everything, Switch Dates were called TWIRPP Dates. TWIRPP stood for "the woman is responsible for planning and paying." To simplify the Switch Date, just switch what you typically do. If your mate usually brings in the paper, you get it. Whoever usually cooks breakfast gets to be served.

Sit in each other's place at the dinner table. If you have children, they may enjoy participating in this dinnertime shuffle. Let each person act like the person in whose place he is sitting. This can be quite revealing. No one—absolutely no one—can imitate parents as well as their own son or daughter!

One benefit of a Switch Date is that it helps you to be more aware of who does what, and it may alert you if one of you should be more involved in helping out the other.

37 ♥ Slumber Party Date

The Idea: If you are looking for cheap and easy dates, there's a good chance you have friends who are too. One couple who fit this description told us about their Slumber Party Date. For us it brought back some fond memories.

We were off on a ski retreat with a group of families and were staying in an old Swiss hotel with high ceilings and squeaking floors. Jonathan was too young to ski, so we took turns skiing. Dave went skiing with our other two sons in the morning, and Claudia skied with them in the afternoon. After the boys skied all day, they ice-skated in the early evening; so they fell quickly asleep after they got ready for bed.

Be Spontaneous: One particular evening another couple put their equally tired kids to bed and came down to our room. We talked and laughed into the wee hours of the night. Finally, we told our friends goodnight and they went back down the hall to their room.

A few minutes later, as we were getting ready for bed, there was a knock on our door. Who should appear but our friends? Their two children had locked them out of the room. Try as hard as they could, they were unable to wake up their kids. So we had a Slumber Party Date. We made a makeshift bed on our floor for our friends and they spent the night with us.

Or Plan to Make It Happen: We didn't anticipate our Slumber Party Date, but other friends planned theirs. Here's what they told us.

"Our Slumber Party Date included two other couples and us. We are all close, longtime friends. All of us were broke and looking for something fun and outrageous to do, so we decided to have a slumber party.

"Everybody brought his own sleeping bag, favorite video movie, bottle of pop, and junk food. We moved our furniture out of the way and had an all-night video party. When people got tired, they went to sleep. It reminded us of being back in high school and going to youth retreats. The next day we had to return to our adult world, but for one night we had a great party!"

It did sound like fun, but we're not sure our backs would make it through the night. We prefer slumber parties for two, but if it rings your bell, plan your own Slumber Party Date. After an all-night party, you'll be all ready for the next part of our fifty-two dates—the "We're Just Too Tired" Dates.

"We're Just Too Tired" Dates

38 ♥ Play-with-a-Pet Date

The Idea: When we get too old and feeble to travel, we're going to get a pet. In the meantime, we enjoy being around the menagerie of cats that belongs to our sons and their wives, Jarrett and Laurie and Joel and Jeanne. Between the four of them, they have five cats! One couple has three, and the other two.

We remember thinking, "What would a young couple in law school want with three cats?" From observing Jarrett and Laurie, we think we know the answer. It makes for inexpensive entertainment—especially when you're too tired to do anything else. Their three feline friends add fun to life.

Regain Emotional Health:
If you are just too tired for the more strenuous dates, you can sit around and play with your animals. Psychologists tell us pets can be therapeutic and good for our emotional health.

When we were first married, we did have a pet—a hamster named Basel. You may not believe this, but Basel was a wedding present! (Claudia's brother has a funny sense of humor.) We did enjoy our pet, but Basel was a problem hamster. He kept breaking out of his cage and chewing the fringe off our chenille bed spreads. (Remember those?)

Consider Alternatives: If you, like us at present, have no furry friends, don't despair. You can still have a Play-with-a-Pet Date. Here are a couple of suggestions:

1. Visit a pet store. One pet store in our town lets the cats that are for sale roam the store. Customers can pet and visit with the cat of their choice.

2. Offer to "sit" your neighbor's pet for an evening. When our boys were growing up, we used to pet-sit for long enough to know who really had to take care of them —and it wasn't our three boys! But a pet for an evening can be fun.

3. Check the phone book for the number of your local animal shelter, Society for the Prevention of Cruelty to Animals (SPCA), or Humane Society. We hear that some animal shelters like for people to come walk the dogs and play with the cats. If this is true in your town, don't rule this out as a fun date when you're too tired to talk to people.

Disclaimer: We assume no responsibility for any pet purchases or adoptions resulting from this date!

39 ♥ Secret TLC Date

The Idea: Working together has its frustrations. Working together at home simply adds to them! Many entrepreneurial couples are now working together out of their homes. We have done this for years and are always looking for tips to survive the pressure of home and business being in the same location. Our friend, Karen, offered a great tip. When the pressure begins to build, slip off and have a Secret Closet Date.

Look for a Chance to Sneak in Some TLC:

"Our secret, spur of the moment date," Karen shared, "is in our walk-in closet. We slip into our closet and close the door. It's one place we can get away, at least briefly, from our three noisy preschoolers. Our closet dates usually last only a few minutes, but hiding from the kids makes it fun and 'forbidden.' Although we do try to go out on dates, these closet dates are inexpensive, convenient, and sneaky. They also give us a large dose of TLC that we both need to get through the day."

You may have to have a Work Together Date of cleaning out the closet before you try this date. I'm not sure we could get in our closet and close the door at the same time! If you don't have a walk in closet, or the time to clean it, try the bathroom.

Find a Secret Place at the Office: Here's a suggestion from Julie for a Secret TLC Date for couples who work outside the home.

"Our offices aren't that far apart, so we ride to work together and park our car about halfway between our two offices. We sometimes plan to take our morning or afternoon break at the same time and meet in the parking lot. What do we do? We park ourselves in our car and snuggle and talk. The time is usually hurried and limited, but it gives us that shot in the arm we need to get through our day."

Take these suggestions or come up with your own Secret TLC Dates. They will help you overcome that feeling of being just too tired.

40 ♥ Bland Date

The Idea: There are times we are all under the weather, but dating in that condition isn't much fun unless you are Brenda and Mike. They've changed the script! (You may remember them as the Blue Highways Daters, page 19.)

Brenda and Mike had both been under a lot of stress. And the stress increased when they discovered one of them had an ulcer. So what did this most unusual couple do? First, they had to slow down. They also had to change their diet, and that's how they came up with this unique date. Since they had to eat bland food, they decided to have a Bland Date.

Plan to Keep It Plain: What do you do on a Bland Date?

"First," Brenda and Mike told a friend of ours, "we wore bland clothes, and what is more bland than beige? Beige matched our bummed-out feeling.

"Next, we listened to bland, very low-key music, like Andy Williams, The Lettermen, and the Carpenters. And we concluded the evening with a slide show of a trip Mike took with his family to Carlsbad Caverns and Los Angeles, when he was fourteen."

Now we're old enough to be fans of Andy and Perry.

We think their music is romantic and not bland at all, but Brenda and Mike are only thirty and thirty-two.

What did they eat on this date? The most bland food they could find—chicken, white rice, baked apples, and vanilla ice cream. Their mild, colorless menu blended perfectly with their clothing!

Our hats are off to Brenda and Mike. We're smart enough to know having a bland date didn't make the ulcer go away, but they proved you can have a fun date even when you don't feel like it. They leave us no room to say, "We're just too sick and tired to date our mate!"

41 ♥ "We're Just Too Tired to Talk" Date

The Idea: Sometimes we are just too tired to talk—or should we say sometimes Dave is too tired to talk. Claudia can always talk. But recently, even Claudia was talked out.

We had just returned from leading Marriage Alive Workshops back-to-back in several different cities, and we were even tired of talking about marriage. We didn't want to see people or do anything that required any energy at all, so we had a "We're Just Too Tired to Talk" Date. This date required no energy because we prepared for it beforehand.

Be Ready to Be Tired: We don't watch a lot of television, but when we are out of town or busy and know we're going to miss a good program or movie, we try to record it so we can watch it when we are home. The problem is we usually never get around to watching the shows we've recorded. You see, we have this bad habit of not labeling the tapes we use and then we record over the very program we want to see. If you've ever done this, you know how frustrating it is.

We finally decided to do something about this. So we created a "We're Just Too Tired to Talk" shelf, where we keep blank tapes, a felt-tip pen, labels, and a section for previously recorded tapes.

Now, when we want to videotape a program, we know

where we can find a tape for recording. We label it and date it before we record, and afterward, we immediately place the tape on our special shelf. As a result, when we are really bummed out, we're prepared for a "Just Too Tired to Talk" Date.

Have Dinner Delivered: Sometimes we order

pizza to eat while we watch our videos. We keep a couple of current pizza coupons on our video shelf so it won't take much energy to find them. Other times we pull out frozen dinners and plop them in the microwave. We don't go out of the house and we don't talk to each other unless we want to. Another tip—we don't answer the phone. Instead, we let the answering machine do the talking.

Consider Another Option: Our friends, Jon

and Maria, told us about their favorite We're Just Too Tired to Talk Date, which does require one last spurt of energy. They go to the video store and then get take-out food from their favorite Chinese restaurant. When they get home, they roll the television and VCR into their bedroom and crawl in bed with their bed trays and Chinese dinner.

They eat, watch movies, fall asleep—whatever they want to do. And they don't talk unless they want to. The next morning life continues with conversation, but one of the things they usually talk about is their relaxing date the night before.

42 ♥ Long Distance FAX-a-Date

The Idea: What do you do when you are on the road and you're tired and lonely? Although we travel a lot together, there are times when one of us is on the road alone. It's not fun—especially over a weekend!

Sometimes you just have to make the best of a situation. That's easier for us now that we have a FAX machine. We may be miles apart, but we've discovered how to FAX-a-Date.

The goal of a FAX-a-Date is to stay in touch. It also gives us something to look forward to. Most hotels have FAX facilities for their guests, so after we've completed our evening speaking engagement or seminar, we are ready to begin having FAX fun!

FAX then Phone: You can use your own creativity, but here are a few ideas to get you started.

- How do I love you, let me FAX the ways _____.

- The funniest thing that happened to me today was _____.

- My most favorite thing about you is _____.

After we've exchanged a couple of FAXes, we follow up with a phone call. Phone calls are nice, but there is something about FAXing notes back and forth that is fun.

Find Other Ways to Stay Close: If you don't have access to a FAX machine, don't rule out this date. There are other ways you can connect and stay in touch. Why not:

- Read the same article or chapter in a book and be prepared to discuss it when you call each other at the end of the day or when you return home.
- Hide a love note in your mate's briefcase, suitcase, or garment bag.
- Watch the same television program and then talk about it.
- Plan your next vacation or a twenty-four hour getaway.
- Talk through your schedule for the next week.
- Plan a special date with each other in the next ten days.

Long Distance Dates encourage us when we are tired and lonely. They keep us in touch and help us to appreciate each other in a new way. But the best part of being separated by the miles is getting on that plane or train or in that car and coming home to our mate. For a great welcome home date see the Limo Date (page 123).

43 ♥ Overcoming the Blahs Date

The Idea: If you're like us, you'll feel just too tired to date when the blahs are getting you down. The weather may be too hot or too cold or too rainy. Your finances may resemble the national debt. Your to-do list may seem endless. That's enough to make anyone tired.

Maybe you need to take time out for an Overcoming the Blahs Date. You can do one of two things.

Chase Away Someone Else's Blahs:

1. Do something to cheer up somebody else. When we get involved in doing something for someone else, the blahs quickly disappear. Consider the following:

- Together with your mate take an evening and call or write someone you haven't contacted in a long time. Recently, we got a letter from an Austrian friend we haven't heard from in years. It made our day.
- Write a note of encouragement to someone you know who is having a problem.
- Make a date to visit a nursing home or hospital. Many people in these institutions rarely get visitors and could use a little encouragement.
- Brighten the life of an elderly friend or relative by making a surprise visit. Call ahead if you're not sure they are up to a surprise.

Step Out of Your Comfort Zone:

2. Do something out of character and unusual. You may want to:

- Try a new recipe—something different from anything you've ever tried before.
- If you have a fireplace, build a fire and roast hot dogs.
- Have a picnic on the living room floor. All you need is a checkered tablecloth, French bread, and cold cuts. Why not put in some colored hard-boiled eggs? This will add some laughter as you chase the blahs away.
- Get out some of your young children's games—Twister is a good one—and play the games together. Or go roller blading, if you haven't already tried this sport.

You may enjoy these dates so much that you find yourself looking forward to the next time a case of the blahs strikes.

44 ♥ Showers, Bubble Bath, and Candles Date

The Idea: Recently, we spoke at a Sweetheart Banquet. As is our custom at the end of our talk, we asked the group to tell us about their favorite dates. When we do this, we usually get the best dating suggestions after the formal program. This time was no exception. One couple stood around until we were alone and then shared the following story.

"When we were first married many years ago, we attended a Marriage Enrichment event where someone shared about how much fun it is to shower together. We tried it and found out they were right. We've been showering together every morning since! We didn't know if we should share that with the whole group."

Take a Water Break: This is a good date suggestion for the times you and your mate are just too tired to do anything else. A shower really soothes and refreshes. Another couple offers this variation.

"We both work long hours. Sometimes when we come home we are totally exhausted. We wouldn't even have the energy to shower together, so here's what we do. Fortunately, we have two bathrooms (and no children yet), so we run each other's baths in separate bathrooms. We add scented bath oil beads or bubble bath—whatever we know our mate likes. We also light candles for each other. Votive candles work great. We turn on soothing music and know we are both in for a relaxing treat.

"It's fun to indulge in the quietness of a warm bath that someone else has prepared for you. We've even decided it's okay if the warm water saps what little energy we might still have. This is a We're Just Too Tired Date so we have no expectations for the evening except to relax and be together. Anything else that happens is totally spontaneous and optional."

Which do you prefer—showers or baths? Maybe you have your own private whirlpool. When you are just too tired, take your pick!

The Best Dates from Marriage Alive Alumni

45 ♥ Hiking Date

The Idea: Our best dates usually have one thing in common—few distractions and lots of conversation. Walking together is a great way to accomplish this. Of course, when walking in the mountains, you are allowed to refer to this activity as hiking. (Calling it hiking also justifies purchasing hiking boots, day packs, and trail mix with chocolate candy!)

Marriage Alive Alumni, Sam and Cindy, love to hike in the Smoky Mountains and have told us about their experiences.

Map Out a Weekend: "One of our favorite hikes starts on Friday night," Sam told us. "That's when we take the kids over to Cindy's parents' house. Her parents also consider this to be somewhat of a wilderness adventure.

"We get an early start on Saturday morning and stop on the way for breakfast. After breakfast, we realize something is missing! No sticky feeling from syrup kisses, no food impregnated on our clothing, and most of all no stares throughout the meal from the entire non-smoking section of the restaurant. We agree that this missing feeling is good and should be encountered on a regular basis.

"Arriving at the trailhead, we begin our four-mile hike along the Appalachian Trail to Charles Bunion. No, this isn't a discount shoe store in Pigeon Forge. It is a scenic overlook which makes a nice spot for lunch. The distance and difficulty also make this an enjoyable day hike. A day pack is all we need to carry water and lunch."

Enlighten Your Loved Ones as You Hike:

"Hiking should be a requirement for all marriages. It provides the husband with the unique opportunity to enlighten his wife through expressions of deep philosophical truths. I can't describe the impact this has on Cindy as I share my analogies to life. 'I think my life is like a mountain spruce, balding from acid rain,' really touches her. She is so moved, at times she can't even look at me. She simply stares up in the sky shaking her head. I must overwhelm her.

"Cindy's only disappointment with our first hiking experience was that there was no hotel along the trail anywhere.

"Being the alert and sensitive husband I am, I suggested we stay overnight in a back country shelter our next trip. Once again, she stared up at the sky and started shaking her head. I did hear her say something about God. I suppose she was thanking Him for me."

By the way, Sam and Cindy just took a refresher Marriage Alive Workshop. We are happy to report their next date will be a romantic date. Cindy agreed to go to any back country shelter that has a jacuzzi!

46 ♥ Breakfast on a Motorcycle Date

The Idea: We have always enjoyed breakfast dates. When our three sons were teenagers, it was a niche of time we found that we could slip out by ourselves and get back home before the first sleepyhead even woke up.

Over the years, we've tried many different places for our breakfast dates, but none were quite as creative as the place Bob and Betty chose.

Bob and Betty are your typical dual career couple with a time crunch life-style that leaves them few opportunities for finding time alone as a couple. Bob decided to do something about it and thus their unique breakfast date.

Create Your Own Place: The day started as an average day. Bob left early for work in order to meet an important deadline—or so Betty thought. After a quick cup of coffee, Betty was on her way to her downtown office. After parking her car, she began the two-block walk to her office. Thinking about her daily agenda, she hardly noticed the commotion at the next intersection.

Then she saw him. There was Bob with his parked motorcycle. But this was not an ordinary parked motorcycle! It had been transformed into a most creative sidewalk cafe!

The motorcycle was covered with a tablecloth, complete with two place settings of dishes, a thermos of coffee, and sweet rolls. Needless to say, this provided laughs for those who walked by, as well as a reminder to spend time with those you love.

You may not own a motorcycle, but don't let that stop you. Plan your own unique breakfast date. Take it from us. It's a great way to start the day!

47 ♥ The Limo Date

The Idea: We will never forget our first ride in a limo. Our first book had just been published, and, as guests of our publisher, we were attending a bookseller's convention in Washington, D.C. The real thrill for these two green writers was sharing the limo ride to the hotel with a seasoned author. Besides recognizing her name, we knew she was seasoned by her luggage. She had only one carry-on!

Limos can add excitement to any date. But they are also expensive, so if you're not running over with money, take our friend's suggestion and improvise.

Economize and Still Have Fun: Judy had spent the entire week at the bedside of her mother. To say the week had been stressful is an understatement. On the flight home, she wondered if her husband, Dan (who is not time oriented), would be there to meet her. Was he ever!

As Judy deplaned, she heard her name on the pager: "Mrs. Roberts, please meet your party at Gate 6."

This is odd, she thought, as she looked around for Dan. About that time she spotted her husband. There he was, complete with a driver's cap and a huge sign that said, "Limo for Mrs. Judy Roberts."

He escorted her to the parking lot. Their station wagon

wasn't exactly a limo, but as Dan loaded her luggage in the back, she felt special anyway.

By the way, they did not go straight home. Instead Dan whisked her away for a surprise date. Where did they go? You'll have to use your imagination!

Several hours later, Judy arrived home, relaxed and ready to catch up with her two teenaged sons, help her ten-year-old daughter with a history project, and eat home-delivered pizza.

48 ♥ Airport Date

The Idea: Airports have always fascinated us. We have experienced some really dramatic and traumatic things at airports.

Four days before our wedding, Claudia met Dave's parents and sister for the first time in the Atlanta Airport. They had flown in from Naples, Italy, where Dave's dad was stationed with the army.

Our most joyous and most tiring airport experience was in the airport at Frankfurt, Germany, back in our army days. Dave, at the invitation of Uncle Sam, arrived in Germany three months ahead of Claudia. Needless to say, we were eager to be together again. Claudia's twenty-four-hour flight was on one of those old army prop planes. It arrived twelve hours late, after stopping for repairs and refueling in Newfoundland. Claudia still remembers wondering if she would make it to Germany.

Our most traumatic airport experience was losing our five-year-old in the Atlanta Airport minutes before we were to board our plane for Vienna where we were living at that time. Another time, as Claudia flew back to Europe with our three young sons, an engine went out causing the flight to return to New York for an emergency landing.

With all our airport traumas, we were naturally curious

when Marriage Alive Alumni, Bill and Jean, told us that their favorite dates were at airports.

Use Your Imagination: "When we were first married, our dating budget was practically nonexistent so we had to rely on our own ingenuity. One thing we loved doing was going to the Detroit Metropolitan Airport to watch people and planes come and go.

"Sometimes we took a snack or soda to have while we people and plane watched. We would rejoice with people whose loved ones were coming home and cry with those whose loved ones were leaving. It was during the Vietnam conflict so there were a lot of sad departures, but also quite a few emotional and joyful arrivals.

"As we watched others, we would fantasize about their destinations and imagine ourselves, traveling to faraway places. We'd wonder what people would be like and what we would do if we were traveling to Florida, Hawaii, Europe, or New York. As young newlyweds with lots of dreams, it was a fun, inexpensive date.

"We're now about to celebrate our twenty-fifth wedding anniversary, and it's still fun to have airport dates. The airports have changed over the years, but people are the same."

49 ♥ Surprise Travel Date

The Idea: One misconception about traveling is that it is always exciting and fun. We must admit at times it can be, but more often than not, life on the road is just living without the conveniences of home and with many added frustrations.

Recently, we were flying to speak at an army installation in Wisconsin. We like to use our time wisely, so we had planned to work on the plane. The only problem was one of us sat in the front of the plane and the other in the back, making it rather hard to communicate.

On the trip home, our flight left Minneapolis late. We were afraid we were going to miss our connection in Memphis. But the connecting flight was two hours late arriving in Memphis.

Fun? That day traveling was about as much fun as cleaning the oven!

Create Your Own Surprise: Some Marriage Alive Alumni, like Jody and Linda, are on the road even more than we are. Jody and Linda are from Texas, but they live in Vienna and travel extensively in Europe and the Orient. They also have to deal with the frustrating little surprises of travel. But on one particular trip, Jody decided to create his own surprise that was anything but frustrating. He planned and pulled off a Surprise Travel Date.

Take a Different Turn: "It was to be a long, long trip. First, we were booked on a flight to London, and then on to Hong Kong. Taking care of last minute details for our month absence from our home in Vienna left me totally exhausted. All I wanted to do on the first leg of our trip was to sleep.

"Imagine my surprise when Jody handed me a homemade card. My creative husband had written me a poem. Now, I said he was creative, not necessarily poetic, but this poem took the prize. He invited me to spend two days alone with him in London.

"Jody had made reservations at a wonderful English inn. He also presented me with tickets for a play we had wanted to see. I felt like he had given me the moon!

Make the Most of the Moment: "The first thing we did after we arrived in London was to take a nap and enjoy the luxury of having no schedule to meet, no one to call, and nothing to do. We just relaxed and enjoyed being together.

"I can't tell you what a difference this Surprise Travel Date made in my attitude about this trip and about life in general. I still savor the memory of Jody's thoughtfulness and the wonderful way he expressed his love and commitment to me on that trip. We highly recommend a Surprise Travel Date to all who can pull it off."

Make It Happen: You may not be traveling to Europe or the Orient, but even if it's only three hours down the road, consider taking your mate along. Since we often travel together doing Marriage Alive Workshops, it's easy to tack on another day or two. It doesn't cost that much more, and what we get from our time alone is well worth it. It's fun if one of you can pull it off as a surprise, but either way, it's a great way to travel. Ask Jody and Linda!

50 ♥ Birthday Treasure Hunt Date

The Idea: Birthday surprises aren't always pleasant! Claudia has never forgotten the year no one remembered her birthday all day long. Claiming she had a headache, Claudia slipped into bed early to end this awful terrible day. No sooner had she fallen asleep, than the doorbell rang. You guessed it. There were all of our friends with a surprise birthday.

Years later, we went away for a weekend to celebrate Claudia's birthday. This may be hard to believe, but Dave actually forgot it was her birthday the day it came. At eleven in the morning, Claudia, tired of feeling angry and rejected, finally told Dave what was bothering her.

Some of our Marriage Alive Alumni, like Judy and Bob, outdo their leaders. Judy described how she suprised Bob with a Birthday Treasure Hunt Date. Here's how she described it.

Create Clues: "It wasn't even Bob's birthday. Actually, it was Sunday afternoon, the day before Bob's birthday, so I would catch him off guard. His first clue that something was up came when I handed him an envelope with a clue inside. My one-of-a-kind poetic clue let him know the hunt was beginning immediately. No need to change clothes—he could proceed to the first location.

"His clues took him all over our neighborhood and a

surrounding four mile radius. One of his clues was a phone call from me that he received in a phone booth. Another clue took him to a grocery store to buy his own birthday balloon.

"The next clue led him to my Dad's home. Laid out for him in their guest bedroom was a change of clothes to dress for dinner. The final treasure stop was our favorite restaurant where I, and two other couples, greeted him. We had a wonderful evening celebrating his birthday together. That was one birthday he didn't even mind getting a year older!"

Choose the Best Time: If your mate has a birthday coming up and he or she likes adventure, consider a Birthday Treasure Hunt Date. Just don't plan it when his or her favorite football, baseball, or basketball team is playing on television. And plan to have this date before bedtime!

51 ♥ Alone and Together Date

The Idea: Is it possible to be too close to your mate? Most couples complain of not having enough time with each other. On the other end of the spectrum are couples like us who are together almost continuously.

At times we simply need a break from each other, so we really appreciated the dating suggestion from Marriage Alive Alumni, David and Susanne. They suggested that we have an Alone and Together Date. This is also a great date for couples who aren't together all the time, but simply need some time alone.

Here's how David and Susanne describe one of their Alone and Together Dates.

Make a Day of It: "One of our favorite dates is an all-day trip to the mountains. We pack a picnic lunch and go to our spot by a stream. We spend most of the afternoon separately. With three small children and a medical practice, our lives are busy, hectic, and at times quite stressful. We both need time alone so this gives us a chance to read, pray, journal, hike, nap—whatever we individually feel like doing.

"Later in the afternoon, we meet back at our spot and share our thoughts, insights, and any discoveries we have made like pretty rocks, flowers, or mushrooms. It's amazing how things come back into perspective when we take time together and alone to reflect and just enjoy being out in nature.

"On the way home, we stop at a favorite restaurant for dinner. Our three children, tired baby-sitter, and hectic pace of life are all waiting for us when we get home; but we have discovered after our Alone and Together Date we are refreshed and ready to face the next challenge."

52 ♥ Ten Bonus Dates for Mates

More Ideas: Because our Marriage Alive Alumni are so creative and have so much fun dating their mates, we couldn't possibly include all their terrific dating suggestions. We have squeezed in as many as possible, however, by condensing ten more dates for mates from our Marriage Alive graduates.

1. "We love to go to a deserted field, take a picnic, and fly kites as we listen to classical music on our boom box." Bob and Cindy

2. "Craft shows and antiquing are our favorite dates. We always try to stop on the way home to watch the sunset." Chip and Susan

3. "Our favorite date was a four-day cruise on the Chesapeake Bay on a chartered thirty-two foot sailboat." Bill and Val

4. "One of our favorite dates is a day away to escape the responsibilities of parenting for a few hours and just to be silly and do whatever we want to do. It's fun to go to a state fair or an amusement park. We love riding the bumper cars." Bill and Donna

5. "Skiing together is fun, exhilarating, and brings color to your cheeks. Don't forget to have a snowball fight!" Jay and Alison

6. "We love the great outdoors and backpacking and camping out." Hans and Barbara

7. "Cooking breakfast at our favorite waterfall is invigorating. If we're early enough, we get to see the sun rise." Greg and Cheryl

8. "After early church, we take the Sunday paper and a picnic lunch on our ski boat. We motor into a deserted cove, put our feet up, read the paper, and just relax." Kent and Susan

9. "We love to go to our favorite little restaurant, order coffee and dessert, and enjoy the live jazz music." Janet and John

10. "We enjoy reliving our first date with each other. We go to the same place we first went together, eat the same food, watch the same movie, and talk about the feelings we shared that day and how we have grown in our relationship since then." Patty and Bill

If this book inspires you to date your mate, we would love to hear from you. Tell us your most fun experiences. You can write to us at:

MARRIAGE ALIVE INTERNATIONAL
P.O. Box 90303
Knoxville, TN 37990

If you like these dates, you'll find more ideas in our recently released book, *The Marriage Track.*

Let us encourage you to go on and date your mate. It will keep your marriage alive, fun, and heading in the right direction!

Dave and Claudia have been married for thirty years and are parents of three adult sons, two daughters-in-law, and five grandkittens.

Together the Arps founded and now direct Marriage Alive International, a marriage and family enrichment ministry. The Marriage Alive Workshop is popular across the United States and in Europe. They also founded the MOM'S and DAD'S Support Groups, which have curriculae for churches and schools.

Claudia is the founder of the MOM's Support Groups, a family enrichment resource program with groups throughout the United States and in Europe. She is also the author of *Beating the Winter Blues* and *Almost 13.* Claudia has a B.S. in Home Economics Education from University of Georgia.

Dave is co-author with Claudia of the *60 One-Minute Marriage Builders* and a family life educator with a B.S. from Georgia Institute of Technology and an M.S. in Social Work from the University of Tennessee.